PRAISE FOR *LEADING THE REBOUND*

Leading the Rebound is a must-read for every leader preparing to restart in-person teaching and learning. The 20+ must-dos create a practical road map that empowers leaders with the insight and confidence needed to focus on implementing the essential recommendations: Acceleration of student learning through instructional excellence, social and emotional needs of students and staff, leveraging strengths from distance learning, are just a few! This will be a welcome and game-changing resource to guide leaders in the challenging next steps of our new instructional normal.

—**Melissa Dutra,** Assistant Superintendent, Santa Maria-Bonita School District, CA

Given the turbulent nature of our times, we are facing a nexus in public education. We need to re-establish our schools' culture that will direct knowledge into wisdom, transform fear into hope and lift isolationism into compassionate engagement. It is more urgent than ever for leaders to be bold and courageous to take back the spirit of public education. *Leading the Rebound* will offer the reader crucial strategies to embark on this critical journey.

—**Francisco Escobedo,** Superintendent, Chula Vista Elementary School District, CA

Leading the Rebound has tackled the most complex and difficult aspects of K–12 education during this unsettling time. This is an authentic and powerful call to action that inspires educators to do all that is necessary to create a school environment in which both students and adults thrive. Ultimately, we are shaping individual futures, and for that reason alone, this resource should be on every educator's bookshelf.

—**Leticia Hernandez,** Assistant Superintendent of Human Resources
National School District, CA

It is time to stop saying we changed something in education because of COVID and start saying we changed this because COVID gave us the opportunity to rethink education. *Leading the Rebound: 20+ Must-Dos to Restart Teaching and Learning* is the perfect book to help districts and schools move forward from the pandemic. The book offers support and guidance on all aspects of the education process, including social and emotional learning; curriculum, instruction, and assessment; classroom management; teacher evaluation and feedback; and parent–teacher–student relationships. Instructional Leadership Teams can utilize this book as a reference to help them identify where their gaps are, consider the reality, the recommendations, redefine and redirect, and agree to commitments. I could not put this down. Books from Fisher and Frey never disappoint and this is no different.

—**Michelle Fitzgerald,** Assistant Superintendent of Curriculum, Instruction,
and Professional Development, Kansas City Public Schools, KS

LEADING THE
REBOUND

LEADING THE
REBOUND

20+ MUST-DOS TO RESTART TEACHING AND LEARNING

DOUGLAS FISHER

NANCY FREY

DOMINIQUE SMITH

JOHN HATTIE

FOR INFORMATION:

Corwin

A SAGE Company

2455 Teller Road

Thousand Oaks, California 91320

(800) 233-9936

www.corwin.com

SAGE Publications Ltd.

1 Oliver's Yard

55 City Road

London EC1Y 1SP

United Kingdom

SAGE Publications India Pvt. Ltd.

B 1/I 1 Mohan Cooperative Industrial Area

Mathura Road, New Delhi 110 044

India

SAGE Publications Asia-Pacific Pte. Ltd.

18 Cross Street #10-10/11/12

China Square Central

Singapore 048423

Director and Publisher, Corwin Classroom: Lisa Luedeke

Editorial Development Manager: Julie Nemer

Content Development Editor: Jessica Vidal

Associate Content Development Editor: Sharon Wu

Production Editor: Melanie Birdsall

Copy Editor: Diane DiMura

Typesetter: C&M Digitals (P) Ltd.

Proofreader: Theresa Kay

Indexer: Sheila Hill

Cover Designer: Gail Buschman

Marketing Manager: Deena Meyer

Printed in the United States of America

ISBN 978-1-0718-5045-9

Library of Congress Control Number: 2021903824

This book is printed on acid-free paper.

21 22 23 24 25   13 12 11 10 9

Contents

Introduction

COVID-19 may have given us the best opportunity to create a new normal of schooling. You have the potential to change the grammar of schooling as we know it and magnify the effective practices from the past while leveraging the lessons learned during pandemic teaching. You have the opportunity to lead the rebound for your school or school system. Think of it as a once-in-a-lifetime chance to improve the systems that serve our students.

Of course, schools need to open safely. The information from public health officials has been incorporated into district and state guidelines, so we will not focus on that advice here. Yes, it is important to ensure the safety and health of our staff and students. But our roles are more complex and require that we also attend to the learning occurring with teachers and students.

We also need to attend to the well-being of our staff and students. Thus, social and emotional learning (SEL) needs to be more prominent in the curriculum and not relegated to an extra-curricular event. We need to rebuild the agency of many of our students and staff. In too many cases, children, youth, and adults have come to believe that their efforts are not making a difference and that anything they do results in failure. As leaders, we may be feeling the same lack of impact. But there are good things happening and we need to harvest those wins and ensure that more success is experienced by educators and students.

Our attention must be focused on prioritizing learning. There is a fairly significant focus on learning loss in the media. There are debates about the amount and truth to these claims, but the fact is that students have things to learn from the experiences that their teachers plan. Our focus should be on learning leaps rather than on learning loss. This requires a careful analysis of current student performance and interventions that accelerate rather than remediate learning. And it requires thoughtful instruction and assessment that are linked to the learning needs of students. Most students will require interventions to be successful, and we have the opportunity to develop and implement new systems of support that result in significant gains for students. In some cases, we need to win back parent support, while in others, we need to maintain the relationships that were forged between parents and teachers during pandemic teaching.

As part of our collective focus on learning, we need to ensure that the environments that are created are supportive of students. Given the length of time some students have been away from physical school, we expect that there may be some problematic behaviors. Some students did not learn or have the opportunity to practice their pro-social skills. Thus, engaging restorative practices will be increasingly important. We just may change the very nature of discipline and help students come to understand the impact that their actions have on others.

> IN TOO MANY CASES, CHILDREN, YOUTH, AND ADULTS HAVE COME TO BELIEVE THAT THEIR EFFORTS ARE NOT MAKING A DIFFERENCE AND THAT ANYTHING THEY DO RESULTS IN FAILURE.

OUR FOCUS SHOULD BE ON LEARNING LEAPS RATHER THAN ON LEARNING LOSS.

There is likely to be an increased focus on the reasons that students cannot learn. As a profession, we often look to outside forces to explain the gaps in learning. Certainly, the impact of poverty, racism, and lack of opportunities to learn is real. But teachers are powerful in changing the learning trajectory of students who they believe will learn. Thus, it is important that we interrupt the tyranny of low expectations, and challenge each other to hold high expectations for students while providing the support for them to achieve. We must develop and implement effective attendance programs and ensure students are engaged in meaningful learning. And we must recognize and confront the cognitive barriers to learning that students face. That requires recognition that students have been punished with grading systems that do not work.

To accomplish all of this, we will need to invest in effective professional learning communities, provide teachers feedback, and be honest about their performance. It's time to focus on teacher learning as well as student learning. Too often, in education, we are waiting to reach agreement with a majority of staff to implement an initiative. The pandemic created opportunities to act quickly in order to implement what research tells us is needed. It taught us how quickly we can act to implement necessary changes. Having said that, it's still important to build consensus and create a positive culture. When staff feel supported and work in a culture of appreciation, the climate contributes to student learning. Together, we can future-proof students and staff so we are ready for any crisis or opportunity that presents itself in the future.

You will notice throughout this book that we include effect sizes when they are available. We draw on the decades of research that John Hattie has collected, known as Visible Learning®. The effect sizes reported in this book are based on meta-analyses, or summaries of research, that identify the power of a specific influence. At this point, there are over 1,800 meta-analyses in John's database, representing more than 300 million students. You can search the database at www.visiblelearningmetax.com for updates on the effect sizes, as John keeps the information current as new meta-analyses are published.

If there ever was a time to step up and lead, it is now. We need you. Your teachers and staff need you. The students in your school need you. There are things that you simply must do to rebound from the crises that society has confronted. Believe in yourself; we believe in you.

Must-Do 1

TAKE CARE OF YOURSELF

REALITY

A return to school presents a host of opportunities and challenges.

RECOMMENDATION

The self-care routines you developed during school closures must be maintained in order for you to lead effectively during a time of change.

Superintendent Francisco Escobedo reminds us that you cannot fill the cup of another if yours is empty. That's an important message and one that has been too often overlooked as leaders lead through change. But burning the candle from both ends, as the saying goes, only works for so long. It's not sustainable. If you take care of yourself, you can lead for the long term.

This is not a self-help book. But we do want to acknowledge that your attitude influences the climate of the school. Teachers and staff members look to their leaders to judge the status of the organization. Lead with confidence. We've got this. Really, we do. Will there be bumps in the road? Of course. But have you ever had a school year without bumps? The return to school promises to be a hopeful yet challenging time.

But back to you. Your well-being is important. There are only so many things that you can control. And you can control your efforts to maintain your physical and mental well-being. A return to school represents disruptions in the routines you have developed during this pandemic. Your work hours may have shifted, and you may already be commuting again, not working from home. The routines of members of your household have changed, too, and their new schedules may be influencing yours.

Ask yourself the following questions:

DO WHAT YOU CAN TO TAKE CARE OF YOURSELF.

➡ **Do I have a morning routine?** Engaging in some regular routines is relaxing as predictable events reduce stress. Maybe you walk or run in the morning. Maybe you have breakfast with your family. Maybe you listen to music. How do you prepare mentally for the day ahead?

➡ **Do I take breaks?** We need breaks to let our thinking settle. In the busy day of a life in the school or the district office, you might overlook breaks.

➡ **Do I eat in a healthy way?** There are all kinds of recommendations out there for eating, from intermittent fasting to several small meals per day. Resist the urge to slip back into old habits of eating at your desk, grabbing fast food, or skipping meals altogether because you're too busy. Do you have a plan and do you stick with it?

➡ **Am I getting enough sleep?** Sleep is restorative and allows us to consolidate our memories. Put yourself to bed at the same time each night if at all possible. If you have trouble sleeping, you may want to consult a professional. And remember, no screens for the last hour before you sleep.

We are not trying to preach to you about self-care. But do what you can to take care of yourself. You and your family and friends, not to mention the people you work with, will benefit from your efforts.

REDEFINE AND REINVENT

You devote enormous energy to accounting for the anticipated changes that a newly defined sense of schooling needs. It's exciting to consider the possibilities of how we can rethink schooling in ways that benefit young people, their families, and their teachers. But without attention to the changes you'll encounter, it's unlikely that you'll be able to accomplish your goals. We'll put it more directly: *Neglecting yourself doesn't make you a better leader.* Without sounding too touchy-feely, sleep and healthy eating and exercise habits are important to our well-being. So is reducing stress. Your turn. What can you do to support your well-being (see Figure 1 on the next page)? Take the time to adjust your wellness plan to reflect the return to school.

 Commitments

➡ Make sure you have good boundaries in place to ensure that you are maintaining your physical and mental health.

➡ Reconceiving school is exciting but also emotionally challenging. Examine your support system so that you can sustain the energy you need to help your school move forward.

➡ You know yourself best. If it's easy for you to slip back into less healthy habits, find a commitment partner who will hold you accountable.

1 MY WELLNESS PLAN

My morning routine

My plan for stress management

My plan for eating in a healthy way

My exercise plan

My plan for getting regular sleep

Source: Adapted from Fisher, D., Frey, N., Smith, D., & Hattie, J. (2020). *The distance learning playbook for school leaders: Leading for engagement and impact in any setting.* Corwin.

Must-Do

2

TAKE STOCK AND FIND THE PATH

REALITY

It seems like the world is in chaos and we're not sure where to start.

RECOMMENDATION

Spend time taking stock and reflecting on the path forward.

There has been much ambiguity in our work of late. Decisions are made, and then reversed, and then made again. We feel unsettled and concerned about many things. Yet we have learned a lot in a fairly short time. The question is, "Where are we now?" And then, "Where are we going?" This will help us get to the next normal—by reframing our thinking from getting "back to business" to imagining what the "next normal" will be like. As we noted in *Rebound, Grades K–12: A Playbook for Rebuilding Agency, Accelerating Learning Recovery, and Rethinking Schools*, those writing about the next normal, mostly in business, describe an arch with several stages (see Figure 2). These stages apply to the leadership work and include the following:

→ **Resolve:** At this first stage, we recognize what is. This includes acknowledgment of what has been lost, what has been gained, and what the world looks like now. We give ourselves permission to mourn the things that are gone, yet we make a decision to move forward.

→ **Relief and resilience:** As we move into this second stage, we experience some relief and mobilize our resilience. We begin to recognize that we can face challenges and that we rely on our personal, professional, and collective assets to protect ourselves from the effects of the stressors that continue to exist.

→ **Return and reopen:** As we reopen schools and return more and more students to physical classrooms, we experience nostalgia, loss, joy, and a range of emotions. We're thrilled to see students repopulate the campus yet recognize that learning environments have changed. Some students did much better with distance learning, academically and socially, and may choose to continue online. Others craved the social interactions of school or needed more support from a teacher. Still others need significant social and emotional support to reengage with learning. As we reopen, we realize that distance, hybrid, hyflex, remote, blended, and simultaneous learning will continue to be options for some, or many, students. This realization—that school will never be the same as we knew it in the before times—can test our resilience and passion. But, if we embrace the possibilities, we can move forward to reimagining schools.

→ **Reimagine:** As we come to terms with the next normal, we start reimagining the ways in which schools can operate. We talk with teachers about students' ownership of their learning and their ability to self-regulate as they choose strategies for learning, seek feedback, and monitor their progress. If we let ourselves, we can get excited about what the future holds and the ways in which these crises can open the doors of possibility for students.

→ **Redefine and reinvent:** As we embrace the possibilities that we imagine, we begin to redefine school and the learning experiences students have, the ways schools operate, and the very idea of schooling itself. We are emboldened and we take action. We recognize the harm that has been done and create new opportunities for ourselves and our students. And hopefully, we never go back to the way that schooling was. We no longer miss those old days, as our impact has grown and we are realizing success. Also, because we are not the same and our students are not the same. We have grown through this experience for better or worse.

2 THE NEXT NORMAL FOR SCHOOLING

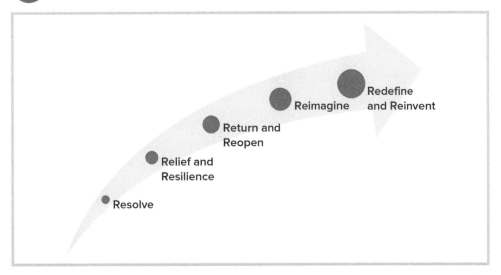

REDEFINE AND REINVENT

It's time to take stock. What are the strengths that you can leverage? What are the needs that have emerged? It's useful to make a list. Literally, make a list of things that are strengths that you can build on and what the needs are that have emerged. For example, you might note any of the following strengths:

- Increased technology proficiency with staff and students
- A large collection of interactive videos
- Strong parent relationships and support
- Improved collaboration and planning on grade-level teams

In addition, you might identify some needs such as the following:

- A group of students who did not attend regularly
- A lack of instructional materials as they were sent home for student use
- Teacher turnover as some have decided not to return

Diagnose and discover where students are in their learning and achievement journey—do not presume or believe that labels or home resources necessarily determine this learning. Be surprised and fascinated to learn what worked well and not for each student and share these stories as a core part of rebounding to better.

To ensure the rebound, we need to build on the strengths while addressing the needs. There are a number of ways to do this. Some people find the use of a logic model helpful as it outlines the resources and activities necessary to achieve the intended results. Figure 3 includes a template for a logic model that can be used to develop a plan that will allow you to lead the rebound.

> TO ENSURE THE REBOUND, WE NEED TO BUILD ON THE STRENGTHS WHILE ADDRESSING THE NEEDS.

3   LOGIC MODEL

OUR INTENDED WORK		OUR INTENDED RESULTS	
RESOURCES	**ACTIVITIES**	**OUTPUTS** *DIRECT BENEFITS*	**OUTCOMES** *INDIRECT BENEFITS*
*If we have access to these resources, **then** these activities can be completed.*			
	*If we successfully complete these activities, **then** these changes will occur as a direct result of the actions.*		
		*If the activities are carried out as designed, **then** these changes will result.*	
			*If participants benefit from our efforts, **then** other systems, organizations, or communities will change.*

Others use goal planning tools to outline what needs to be accomplished. The key is to be clear and remain focused. If we get too distracted, we lose sight of the goals and then do not accomplish them. A sample goal planning tool can be found at resources .corwin.com/DLPlaybook-leaders.

✳ Commitments

➡ Take stock of the strengths and needs of your organization. It's a good starting place.

➡ Develop a plan to address the needs that you have identified.

➡ Stay focused on your goals and share them with others.

Must-Do 3

REBUILD TEACHER AGENCY

REALITY

Many (perhaps most) teachers no longer see the relationship between their effort and the impact that they have.

RECOMMENDATION

Make the link between effort and outcome explicit to rebuild teacher agency.

Prior to the pandemic, most teachers saw the through-line between their efforts and the impact that they had on students and their colleagues. They could see their students' faces and know they were learning. They could walk around the classroom and peek over a shoulder to check for understanding. The vast majority of teachers had a high level of agency, or the belief that what they did mattered. When they invested time in terms of lesson design, teaching, assessing, and so on, good things happened.

Pandemic teaching and, to some extent, distance learning had a destabilizing impact on teachers. Many experienced students who did not engage in learning and students who were failing or, for any number of reasons, did not get online for classes. They taught to empty screens and experienced a profound sense of isolation. As this occurred, teacher agency declined. Over time, teachers attributed the lack of success to their efforts. In other words, they took it personally. As one teacher said, "Nothing I do really matters, so I don't spend a lot of time planning anymore. I just show up and talk to my computer like I am required to." Another teacher said, "I can't really have an impact because some parents are over helping and others are just not there." With reduced agency comes reduced effort and, eventually, demoralization and departure from the profession.

This is really not a good situation for our profession. And leaders are not immune to this either. You, personally, may have experienced a reduction in agency. You may have experienced frustrations or failures and attributed them to your efforts. And thus your agency, well-being, motivation, and willingness to reengage may have suffered. We hope that your colleagues can help you rebuild your own agency. And we hope that you will work to rebuild the agency of the teachers in your organization.

> **YOU, PERSONALLY, MAY HAVE EXPERIENCED A REDUCTION IN AGENCY.**

REDEFINE AND REINVENT

There are at least three ways to rebuild teacher agency.

First, ensure that teachers have opportunities to collaborate with other teachers. When teachers have time to tell their stories and talk shop, including the strategies and practices they are using, their sense of professionalism grows. That's why professional learning communities, professional learning sessions, and time in grade-level or department meetings are important. We need to give teachers time with each other so that they have the opportunity to collaborate and share. Of course, sharing war stories and one-upping each other about how bad things are won't help. Conversations about what students need to learn, how we will move learning forward, who learned what, and what we can do for those who still need to learn feed teachers' souls.

Second, teachers need feedback. In fact, they crave feedback. We all want to know how we are doing and where we can improve. We are not looking for criticism or false praise. Humane, growth-producing feedback is valuable and helps teachers develop in a supportive environment. As we have noted, the best way to ensure that feedback is accepted is to focus on the feedback that the person asks for. So, ask the teacher what they'd like you to look for. Allow the teacher to identify the focus. The point here is that the feedback teachers receive reinforces their sense of efficacy. It's not, yet, about the impact on students. That will come next. It's about the professional conversations that coaches and leaders have with teachers that include recognition of the effort and the appreciation for a job well done.

Third, teachers want to know that they had an impact. They want to see that their work matters. At this point, many teachers have experienced a number of failures. They probably have also experienced a number of successes, but it seems that most people are focused on the failures. Your job is to reestablish the link between effort and impact. Evaluative thinking—the decisions we make in the act of preparing, teaching, and reflecting on our teaching—is at the heart of our profession. Emphasize their evaluative thinking in professional conversations: Value the thinking and we value the teacher. And it's okay to start small. Yes, we all want deep learning for our students and great levels of academic learning. But, when you are working to rebuild teacher agency, small wins are a good place to start. We think of this as harvesting the wins. The key here is to attribute the success or impact to a specific effort of the teacher. Consider the following sentence frames:

> ➡ When you _____, I saw _____. For example, "When you modeled your writing process, I saw a lot of students ask questions and then get to work on their own pieces."

> ➡ Because of your effort to _____, the following happened. For example, "Because of your effort to ensure that every student had a role in the group, students completed the task and we both saw the evidence of learning."

> ➡ Students did _____ because of you. For example, "The students in your class had a partner conversation because you showed them a video of other students doing it."

This last point is really important. We need to change the structure of these interactions. In the past, we may not have needed to make the explicit link between effort and impact. We do now. It's not, "Your students did a good job" or "You modeled well" or even "The learning intentions and success criteria were very clear and linked with the standards." These statements need to acknowledge the specific effort made by the teacher and the success that resulted. And, at least in the short term, teachers need to hear a lot of these.

If we can rebuild teacher agency, we can contribute to the emotional well-being of educators and reduce demoralization and burnout. In fact, we may even save a few teachers from leaving the profession. And we can slowly focus on bigger successes. Just maybe we will reach new levels of learning for teachers and students because of our efforts to ensure that people know that their work is valued and is of value.

WE NEED TO ACKNOWLEDGE THE SPECIFIC EFFORT MADE BY THE TEACHER AND THE SUCCESS THAT RESULTED.

✳ Commitments

> ➡ Configure the schedule to ensure quality time for teachers to collaborate to think aloud about their teaching.

> ➡ Provide growth-producing feedback that teachers ask for on a regular basis.

> ➡ Harvest wins on a daily basis and attribute success to the teachers' effort and expertise.

Must-Do 4

REBUILD COLLECTIVE TEACHER EFFICACY

REALITY

While some teacher teams thrived, others did not.

RECOMMENDATION

Rebuild teams' working capacity and search for evidence of impact.

Collective responsibility is foundational for collective efficacy to thrive. Collective responsibility is defined by Learning Forward across five dimensions (Hirsch, 2010, p. 2):

1. All staff members share a commitment to the success of each student.

2. We do not allow any single teacher to fail in their attempt to ensure the success of any one student.

3. Our students benefit from the wisdom and expertise of *all* teachers in a grade level or subject rather than just their own teachers.

4. Our teachers feel a responsibility to share what is working in their classrooms with their colleagues.

5. Teachers with less experience realize that other teachers are invested in their success and the success of all students.

IN SCHOOLS WHERE THERE IS A HIGH DEGREE OF COLLECTIVE RESPONSIBILITY FOR ACADEMIC SUCCESS AND FAILURE, STUDENTS THRIVE.

If a group does not believe that it is their responsibility to move learning forward, student achievement suffers. In schools where there is a high degree of collective responsibility for academic success and failure, students thrive. You might ask how this would even be possible—Don't we all feel responsible for our students' learning? But consider how often you have heard educators blame their students (or their families) for not learning. We hear people use poverty, motivation, even screen time as reasons why students don't learn. We are not dismissing these as unimportant. But keep this in mind: collective teacher efficacy, with an effect size of 1.39, is nearly three times as influential as socioeconomic status (0.52) on student achievement.

REDEFINE AND REINVENT

Collective efficacy is collective responsibility in action. Collective responsibility is important but not sufficient. Without action, collective responsibility devolves to collective guilt. Collective efficacy requires actions that are purposeful and designed to yield results. Teams that enjoy a high degree of collective efficacy are able to set goals for themselves, pursue them, gauge their progress, make changes as needed, and evaluate their impact. When highly efficacious teams proliferate across a school, the organization becomes efficacious. The culture of the school shifts in material ways, and students and families benefit. What actions are we compelled to take on behalf of students? Use the planning tool in Figure 4 to assist your teams in taking action to improve learning for each student.

4 COLLECTIVE TEACHER EFFICACY PLANNING TOOL

Goals	Proposed Action	Internal Supports We Will Need	External Supports We Will Need	Date to Revisit (Monitor Progress)
To improve equitable access to content				
To improve teacher clarity				
To improve teacher credibility				
To strengthen expectations				
To remove organizational or institutional barriers				

Source: Fisher, D., Frey, N., & Smith, D. (2020). *Teacher credibility and collective efficacy playbook.* Corwin.

❋ Commitments

➡ Rethinking schools requires a collective effort, not just the leader's effort. Rebuild collective responsibility by building the conditions needed to do so.

➡ Collective responsibility must be linked with action in order to result in collective teacher efficacy. Assist teams in defining goals and pair these with the internal and external resources they need.

Must-Do 5

FOREGROUND SOCIAL AND EMOTIONAL LEARNING

REALITY

A major takeaway from pandemic teaching is that we cannot afford to relegate social and emotional learning to the sidelines.

RECOMMENDATION

Infuse social and emotional learning into the academic and non-academic curriculum.

The sudden switch to distance learning and its later variants, including hybrid and simultaneous learning, highlighted a profound need: regular connections to students. In the months that followed, teachers got really creative about ways to include emotional check-ins with students. There were intentional efforts for students to name their emotions, explore their knowledge of self, and foster connections with peers across virtual spaces. All of these were important in a time where human connection was at a premium and socialization opportunities were reduced. It just wasn't enough.

Although we applaud the intentionality of teachers to make these efforts, it was still seen as a largely separate task. Many of these emotional check-ins at the beginning of class were really just a warm-up activity. Rarely were these linked in any way to the learning of the academic lesson. Although these few minutes were appreciated and of some solace, their overall social and emotional learning didn't change much, especially as learning away from the classroom introduced new stressors for your students (and teachers).

SEL PROGRAMS THAT ARE FULLY INTEGRATED INTO THE CURRICULUM AND SCHOOL CULTURE HAVE A MUCH LARGER EFFECT.

The evidence on social and emotional learning is useful but also reflects unrealized potential. Social skills programs, in general, have an effect size of 0.36, suggesting that they are likely to have a positive impact on learning. However, the design and implementation of these programs are important mediators. Those that are implemented as somewhat stand-alone lessons with less connection to the academic flow of the classroom and school have a smaller effect, while those more fully integrated into the curriculum and school culture have a much larger effect. This should come as no surprise, as in general, skills taught in isolation but rarely used are not going to gain breakthrough results.

We need to be careful that we do not add a new role for our teachers, that of school counselors. The teacher's major role is to focus on the social and emotional learning of our students—a sense of confidence to take on learning challenges, feeling invited and safe in this place called *school*, experiencing happiness and joy when learning, and motivated to engage in learning. Where there are social and emotional needs beyond this, we may need to introduce professionals who can work with children and families. Schools were never intended to solve everything.

In truth, we are teaching social and emotional skills even when we don't think we are. We promote a set of values, for better or for worse, through our instruction and curriculum. The Aspen Institute (2019) reminds us that "how we teach is as instructive as *what* we teach. Just as the culture of the classroom must reflect social belonging and emotional safety, so can academic instruction embody and enhance these competencies and be enhanced by them" (p. 13). A classroom grading system that is competitive in nature sends the tacit message to students that it is every person for themselves, and there is no advantage to collaboration. Curricula that are devoid of discussion about how characters exhibit courage, face challenges, or wrestle with ethical dilemmas don't allow young people to integrate these skills into their own lives. In fact, when selecting texts, teachers should consider the ways in which they can integrate discussions of social and emotional issues alongside the academic content.

REDEFINE AND REINVEST

Chances are very good that you already have some teachers at your site who are brilliant at integrating social and emotional and academic learning. If so, that is a great first step. There can also be a temptation to just pile on lots of professional learning and hope for the best. But silos of excellence are not sufficient for rethinking school. To do so requires a systematic approach. We support a four-step approach developed by Jones and colleagues to develop and implement a schoolwide social and emotional and academic learning initiative (2018).

The first action is to use data to guide decision making. Some data may be already available, such as those gathered in measures of school health and safety. However, as we come off an interrupted school year, those data may not reflect the current status. Teacher, staff, student, and family focus groups are likely to be a better source of data and can provide the immediacy you require. Ask them questions about culturally sustaining curricula and their experiences with regard to access to mental health and counseling services and their school discipline experiences.

A second action is to recruit key stakeholders for the process. True integration of principles of social and emotional learning requires the involvement of teachers, of course. But there are other dimensions of schooling, and certificated staff, athletic coaches, and after-school staff are invaluable. Students and families are at the center, and therefore their voices are invaluable for building such an initiative. Equipped with the data gathered through student surveys, focus groups, and family questionnaires, ask these key stakeholders to react to the data. Ask them what they find surprising, confirming, and worrisome. In particular, ask them what's missing. Children are especially insightful about seeing things that are hidden in plain sight.

A third action is to develop specific and measurable needs and goals so that you can adequately monitor progress. As noted in the introduction, the development of a logic model is useful for planning, implementing, and refining a complex initiative. Many use a SMART goal template to create them: specific, measurable, attainable, results oriented, and time bound.

Fourth, based on the data gathered, the stakeholders recruited, and the goals developed, you're ready to select a program or approach. You'll notice we haven't said anything about a social and emotional learning (SEL) framework (there are many) or a program (there are lots of good ones). In many cases, you may find that a free or commercial program is a good springboard for customizing your initiative. And that's exactly the point. There isn't a one-size-fits-all program or approach, and evidence-based ones will tell you the same. In fact, they need to be customized to better meet your school's goals and to capitalize on existing strengths. The key is to integrate social and emotional learning into the academic learning that students do.

WE NEED TO BE CAREFUL THAT WE DO NOT ADD A NEW ROLE FOR OUR TEACHERS, THAT OF SCHOOL COUNSELORS.

✳ Commitments

→ Allow social and emotional issues to become a legitimate narrative across your school and commit to being the school's best listener-detective.

→ Commit to data-informed decision making and be courageous in adhering to it.

→ Gather key stakeholders to develop, critique, and monitor your social and emotional and academic learning initiatives.

→ Customize whatever program or approach you select to meet the needs and strengths of your school site.

Must-Do

6

CHANGE THE LEARNING LOSS NARRATIVE

REALITY

The widespread discussions about learning loss result in deficit thinking and grant permission to lower expectations.

RECOMMENDATION

Change the narrative to focus on *accelerating learning*.

We are not certain about how much learning was lost or for whom. There are students whose performance or understanding has been compromised. Yet there are other students who performed well, even better than in their past. The predictions of learning loss, such as the "COVID slide" projected by the Annenberg Institute at Brown University (Kuhfeld et al., 2020a) of 32 percent to 37 percent in reading and 50 percent to 63 percent in mathematics, have been challenged by large-scale data presented by groups such as NWEA and their 4.4 million MAP assessments of Grades 3 to 8 that show relatively little loss for those who took the assessment (Kuhfeld et al., 2020b). But there is solemn news within those findings. Up to 25 percent of the students who took the test in 2019 did not do so in 2020. Many of those students were from low-income households, often Black or Latinx. While some students did well, others fell further behind. In many school systems, existing equity gaps further widened. The distribution of learning, and learning loss, has not been equal. It wasn't evenly distributed pre-pandemic, either.

The learning loss could be quite different across subjects, and early research hints at some important drops in student writing growth (writing, not handwriting) and may be greater in some areas than others. Don't just assume; have a scouting of where and for whom there may be loss. At the same time, check for accelerated growth as these cases could prove the most worthwhile intel on what worked well to consider in the rebound.

What is clear is that there is a perception of loss and lack of learning. And that perception is fueling conversations about remediation. And that perception is creating a mindset that we need to expect less from students. In fact, there are discussions occurring about not expecting students to learn as much for the next couple of years. That's a dangerous road that leads to further inequity. We need to counter this narrative yet not dismiss the very real concerns about the experiences that students had.

> AS PART OF LEADERSHIP, WE HAVE TO COUNTER THE "LEARNING LOSS" NARRATIVE.

REDEFINE AND REINVENT

Whatever the data are, the students in your school are where they are. It's your role to engage in instructional leadership and ensure that students are learning. As part of that leadership, we have to counter the "learning loss" narrative. If you really think about it, the phrase is mostly wrong. Learning loss implies that they had it and now they don't. The reality is that some students experienced less than ideal instruction and did not learn all that they could have. And yet, some students learned more than they would have.

As learning loss is discussed, we need to focus on acceleration and learning recovery. Drawing on the research regarding acceleration for students identified as gifted and talented, focus conversations on the following:

➤ **Identify skills and concepts that have yet to be learned**.

- What tools do we have to notice what students still need to learn?

- How can we ensure that we do not focus instructional time on content students have already learned?

➡ **Provide key aspects of knowledge in advance of instruction**.

- How can we use what we have learned about asynchronous learning to build background knowledge and vocabulary?

- What content can be previewed before synchronous learning time?

➡ **Increase the relevance of students' learning**.

- How can we capture students' attention and interest and ensure that they see the value in the things that they are learning?

- Can our students answer the question "Why am I learning this?"

➡ **Create active, fast-paced learning experiences**.

- Can we develop lessons that move quickly, perhaps cycling through information several times, and allow students to engage?

- How can we ensure that students are active and practice as part of our lessons?

➡ **Build students' confidence.**

- Are the students building their confidence in their learning as that helps build competence?

- What successes do students have that we can celebrate?

- How can we learn to be strength-spotters rather than deficit-describers?

The effect size of acceleration is 0.68, well worth the effort to change the narrative. Acceleration does not only mean skipping a grade (and the opposite, retention back a year, is among the most systematically negative influences that we know) but can also mean telescoping or ensuring only the core and key parts of the curriculum are covered more deeply. Of course, the narrative needs to be supported with high-quality learning experiences that have an impact. Later in this book we will focus on instruction and intervention. But the fact IS that teachers are very good at achieving the expectations that they have for students, high or low. And teacher expectations have been impacted by the conversations about learning loss.

> RETENTION BACK A YEAR IS AMONG THE MOST SYSTEMATICALLY NEGATIVE INFLUENCES THAT WE KNOW.

✳ Commitments

➡ Do not assume students have, or have not, learned. Diagnose, discover, investigate the status of learning for every student.

➡ Check a broad spectrum from achievement, interest and motivation, angst and loneliness, and health and happiness.

➡ Discuss opportunities for acceleration with your teams.

Must-Do 7

GUIDE TEACHER CLARITY

REALITY

Too much focus is placed on completing tasks and assignments rather than what students are learning and what success looks like when doing these tasks and assignments.

RECOMMENDATION

Support teachers to identify and communicate learning expectations and success criteria.

Students who know what they are learning and know when "good is good enough" (success criteria) are much more likely to actually learn it. Simple enough. In fact, the effect size of having learning goals is 0.51, above the average in terms of impact. Unfortunately, school is too often focused on the task at hand rather than what we will learn from the task. In some cases, this was worsened in pandemic teaching when students were assigned a lot of work to do on their own, especially in asynchronous learning situations. In many cases, they had no idea what they were supposed to be learning or what success looked like, other than getting it done.

To identify what students need to learn, teachers must analyze standards and identify concepts and skills. In particular, they need to determine the cognitive complexity of tasks and optimal learning strategies and tailor instruction to ensure students are taught the best ways of thinking and learning while attending to the concepts and skills. When educators are aware of the grade-level content expectations, they can assess what students already know and where the focus of learning needs to be. In this way, we can recover learning and ensure that instruction is aligned with learning needs. In many places, there are guidelines about which standards should receive priority attention. In other places, it's left to individual districts, schools, and teachers. The art for teachers is to ensure individual students attain these priority concepts and skills. Regardless, if we can ensure that students know what it is they are learning, they're much more likely to learn it, and then their future teachers won't have to keep trying to reteach it.

REDEFINE AND REINVENT

We have argued that students need to know the answer to three questions for each lesson:

 What am I learning today?

Why am I learning it?

How will I know that I have learned it?

The first question focuses on the learning intentions. And note that it says *today*, not this week or this semester. Students need to know what they are learning every day, and each day should expand that learning. Teachers need to communicate learning intentions to students at some point in the lesson. We did not say at the outset of the lesson, but rather at some point. Students should not have to guess or infer; they should be informed.

The second question focuses on relevance. We noted the importance of relevance in accelerating learning. Do students understand the ways in which the information will be used? Do they know when and how they will apply this knowledge? Do they get a chance to learn about themselves and their own learning strategies? If the answer is yes to any of these questions, students are more likely to experience relevance.

The third question focuses on success. What does it mean to learn something? At what level is success measured? When students can talk about their learning and know how they will know if they have learned something, ownership and responsibility for learning are transferred to students. For students to answer this question, they need to know the success criteria. And they may be invited to co-construct success criteria with their teachers. Importantly, the answer is not how my teacher will know that I have learned, but rather how *I* will know that I have learned.

To recover learning, teachers need time with their colleagues to analyze the standards, sequence learning, and develop learning intentions and success criteria. In addition to time, they need examples of learning intentions and success criteria, which were provided in *Rebound* so we will not repeat them here.

Instead, we want to focus on your role as a leader. As you interact with teachers and students, ask them the clarity questions. Keep track of the percentage of teachers and students who can answer them. You may want to support individual teachers if they or their students are unable to answer. Or you may want to send out aggregate data weekly and invite teachers to set goals to increase the percentage of students who can answer these questions.

Imagine the difference in your school if the following happened:

> ➜ Teachers analyzed standards and understood key concepts and skills required by grade-level and content area.

> ➜ Teachers determined what students already knew and did not spend time on that content.

> ➜ Teachers identified the smaller group of students who had gaps in their knowledge and taught them the specific skills or concepts needed for the current unit of instruction.

> ➜ Teachers selected instructional materials and instructional interventions aligned with what students needed to learn.

> ➜ Teachers shared learning intentions, relevance, and success criteria with students such that students talked about their own learning.

> ➜ Students identified where they were in mastering the success criteria and what learning they still needed to do.

Doing this is a game changer. Just how much learning could occur if that were the case? It's within your reach to ensure this happens for every student.

✳ Commitments

> ➜ Provide time and tools for teachers to analyze standards.

> ➜ Develop a shared agreement that teachers share learning intentions, relevance, and success criteria with students daily.

> ➜ Talk with students about their learning, reflect on what it means when students can and can't answer the clarity questions, and develop plans to ensure more can.

TO RECOVER LEARNING, TEACHERS NEED TIME WITH THEIR COLLEAGUES TO ANALYZE THE STANDARDS, SEQUENCE LEARNING, AND DEVELOP LEARNING INTENTIONS AND SUCCESS CRITERIA.

8

ENSURE INSTRUCTIONAL EXCELLENCE

REALITY

Instruction has become more complex as blended learning approaches are becoming part of the classroom flow. Some instructional approaches work better than others. But some educators don't know what works best or how to know, and some are nervous about deviating from their well-used current methods.

RECOMMENDATION

Know what quality instruction looks like across platforms by refining your look-for and listen-for skills. Support teachers to enact instruction that ensures learning and to change practices if students are not learning.

Classroom instruction shouldn't look the same as it did in 2019. The digital competencies gained by students and teachers should remain sharp, and the best of these practices should become a part of the instructional flow of learning in the regular classroom. The danger, however, is that the return to school will devolve to a business-as-usual mindset. The relief from the resumption of face-to-face teaching can lull educators into a false sense of security. The temptation to fall back into old patterns is strong. In truth, things weren't always instructionally satisfactory pre-pandemic.

Teachers' assumptions about their learners and their practice are strongly held, and "shifting teachers' educational imaginations" is not easily accomplished (Segall, 2020, p. 3). Short-term exposure to new ideas and ways of teaching doesn't often lead to transformative change. It takes a longer period of sustained practice to do so. The disruption caused by an unsettled year of schooling may be the catalyst for doing so—but only if we are willing to capitalize on our learning by bridging how it is that we talk about instruction in the context of learning.

> TEACHERS' ASSUMPTIONS ABOUT THEIR LEARNERS AND THEIR PRACTICE ARE STRONGLY HELD.

REDEFINE AND REDIRECT

Observations of classroom instruction are more complex when students are working across platforms. It should be expected that in a given observation, you might see some students working virtually with others or independently, while others are in direct contact with the teacher, and others are working off-line without the teacher. The dynamic and fluid nature of instruction means that a lesson is likely to encompass a number of instructional moves. Know what to look for and listen for so that you can promote teacher thinking and reflection.

Teacher demonstration. Demonstrations provide students with explicit instruction of what they will do or learn. There are a number of ways teachers can demonstrate skills or concepts for students, including direct or explicit instruction, think-alouds and think-alongs, and short lectures. These should be clear and concise so as not to erode into a passive experience for students. Take note of the look-fors and listen-fors in Figure 5 when a teacher is demonstrating a skill or concept.

Collaborating with peers. Peer collaboration and discussion is a linchpin of student learning. In particular, discussion, with an effect size of 0.82, speeds learning. However, this is more than just putting desks or screens together and hoping they'll talk about something. The task design itself is crucial and should promote student collective efficacy and intellectual independence. As we noted in *Rebound*, we recommend a goal that 50 percent of the instructional minutes, averaged each week, should be devoted to students collaborating and interacting with their peers. Not 50 percent consecutive minutes, but a goal that ensures that there is a lot more talk in the classrooms. They also may need to be taught specific skills to contribute to groups and to build confidence to not only engage with the group but believe that the group can arrive at better learning than any individual (including them) (Hattie et al., 2021).

LOOK-FORS AND LISTEN-FORS IN DEMONSTRATION

Pacing	• The time allotted for demonstration is developmentally appropriate. • The demonstration is concise and makes efficient use of time. • The pace of the lesson is steady and consistent.
Rigor and Alignment	• The demonstration is grade appropriate and aligned with standards or expectations for learning.
Statement of Goals	• The demonstration includes a statement of the goal for the lesson. • The teacher names the skill, concept, or strategy being demonstrated.
Explanations and Examples	• Explanations are clear and developmentally appropriate. • Examples and non-examples illuminate the skill or concept being taught.
Modeling	• The demonstration includes modeling of the skill or concept and the decisions made to use it.

Source: Fisher, D., Frey, N., & Hattie, J. (2020). *The distance learning playbook: Teaching for engagement and impact in any setting.* Corwin.

6 **LOOK-FORS AND LISTEN-FORS IN PEER COLLABORATION**

Discussion	• Students have opportunities to engage in discussion in the live session. • The discussion is aligned with the academic learning in the session.
Routines	• The collaboration routine is familiar to students. If the routine is newer to students, it is accompanied with explicit instruction and modeling of the routine. • The collaboration routine used is developmentally appropriate.
Monitoring	• Student thinking is observed and monitored by the teacher. • The teacher provides affirmations and redirection when needed. • The teacher and students provide feedback to one another about the collaboration.
Task Design	• The task or problem is designed to promote intellectual interdependence. • The task is designed so that students use interpersonal skills and communication to successfully collaborate.
Links to Learning	• Students set goals before a collaborative task and monitor their success after the task. • Students are asked to draw conclusions and make connections to new or prior knowledge.

Source: Fisher, D., Frey, N., & Hattie, J. (2020). *The distance learning playbook: Teaching for engagement and impact in any setting.* Corwin.

Coaching and facilitating. Scaffolded instruction during small group learning can result in important advancements in learning. It is important to note that it isn't the small group itself that accomplishes this, but rather the teacher's careful use of prompts and cues to extend students' cognitive range. Attend to the task design during this phase of instruction, too. The task should be challenging, as the teacher is there to provide those important scaffolds.

 ## LOOK-FORS AND LISTEN-FORS DURING COACHING AND FACILITATING STUDENT LEARNING

Grouping	• The students are grouped according to a similar instructional need.
Goals	• The goals of the lesson are stated at the beginning and revisited at the end so that students can monitor their success.
Rigor	• The content of the lesson is complex and challenging for students. • The content of the lesson is grade appropriate and aligned to standards or expectations.
Scaffolding	• The teacher used prompts and cues whenever possible to facilitate a cognitive lift on the part of learners. Students do the majority of explaining, making connections, and asking questions. • The teacher notices students' needs and is responsive, while fostering the independence of students whenever possible.

Source: Fisher, D., Frey, N., & Hattie, J. (2020). *The distance learning playbook: Teaching for engagement and impact in any setting.* Corwin.

Deliberate practice. This might arguably be the big game changer in ensuring instructional excellence. In pre-pandemic schooling, leaders rarely paid much attention to in-class independent work and out-of-class homework. Instead, the focus was solely on what the teacher was doing. But the instructional moves that foster practice are a critical part of learning. Note we say "deliberate" and not just practice, as this involves teaching students to seek and interpret feedback as they practice; otherwise, some will practice the wrong stuff! Rather than simply viewing the learning management system or watching a group of students complete an independent task, talk with the teacher and the students about their knowledge of and dispositions toward practice.

Link instructional moves to student learning. Instructional moves are just that—they are the evaluative thinking that leads to teacher behaviors and actions. This decision making behind why they do what they do and when they choose to do it lies at the heart of teaching. There should be reciprocity between teaching and learning. Simply checking off all the boxes of a "good lesson" isn't sufficient unless we're also attending to evidence of student learning. If the student has not learned, then the teaching did not work.

> WE RECOMMEND A GOAL THAT 50 PERCENT OF THE INSTRUCTIONAL MINUTES, AVERAGED EACH WEEK, SHOULD BE DEVOTED TO STUDENTS COLLABORATING AND INTERACTING WITH THEIR PEERS.

8 **LISTEN-FORS FROM TEACHERS AND STUDENTS ABOUT DELIBERATE PRACTICE**

Teacher Knowledge and Decision Making on Practice	• Students have been taught about the role of practice in their learning. • The practice work is based on student learning data, including student feedback. • Practice work includes opportunities for students to set goals and self-assess.
Teacher Habits and Dispositions About Practice	• Submitted practice work is accompanied by timely teacher feedback, usually within one week. • Student performance on practice work is used to inform future instruction. • A student who struggles to complete practice work is not labeled as "unmotivated" but rather receives additional support to build practice habits.
Student Knowledge About Practice	• Students know about the role of practice in their learning. • They view practice as being more than just a form of compliance. • Students know about the benefits of spaced and deliberate practice.
Student Habits and Dispositions About Practice	• Students set practice goals for themselves. • Students engage in self-assessments that narrow their focus on what needs to be practiced. • Students need to seek and interpret feedback about their work and thinking during practice.

Source: Fisher, D., Frey, N., & Hattie, J. (2020). *The distance learning playbook: Teaching for engagement and impact in any setting.* Corwin.

When you're meeting with a teacher who will be planning a lesson for you to observe, use questions to mediate the teacher's thinking and orient them toward the learning by using the four cognitive coaching questions for planning (Costa & Garmston, 2015):

1. What is a near-term goal that you have for your students or for yourself?

2. What might success look like or sound like? How will you know the lesson was successful?

3. What are some strategies that you have used before that might be successful with this group? What are your hunches?

4. What is most important for you to pay attention to in yourself?

After you have observed the lesson, ask these powerful questions to orient the teacher back to student learning:

➡ In what ways was the lesson you *planned* different from the lesson you *taught*? (Costa & Garmston, 2015).

➡ Could your students at the end of the lesson teach the skills and concepts to other students? This is a powerful exit ticket for you and the students; if they can, it shows a mastery of the concepts and skills you have taught them.

Using mediating questions before and after the observed lesson deepens the conversation beyond the technical skills of teaching to the decision making necessary to cause learning.

✳ Commitments

➡ Hone your observational skills by knowing what you are looking for and listening for in face-to-face, blended, and virtual learning environments.

➡ Pay close attention to the level of teacher talk relative to student talk. Peer collaboration and small group coaching and facilitating are prime times for student discussion.

➡ Transform classroom observations by asking questions that mediate teacher reflection before and after lessons to glean insights into their decision making.

➡ Focus the conversations you have with teachers about the impact of their instructional decisions and talk more about learning than teaching.

USE ASSESSMENTS FOR A RANGE OF PURPOSES

Must-Do 9

REALITY

Despite the critical importance of assessment in learning, these practices are sometimes viewed as "taking time away" from instruction.

RECOMMENDATION

Integrate assessments *for*, *as*, and *of* learning to ensure greater relevance.

Mention assessment in the past and you might have heard grumbles from teachers. Many of the complaints circled around the instructional time "lost" to administering tests, often district-, state-, or provincial-level ones. However, the assessment landscape is far more nuanced than the large-scale ones that often first leap to mind. The vast majority of assessments administered are teacher-based ones. These are classroom practices that are used to check for understand and measure proficiency. These, coupled with standards-based tests, provide a wealth of information for students and teachers. But only if we use them that way.

Many educators gained a new appreciation for the vital nature of assessment in the learning process during distance learning. This is because the focus switched more to the value of the interpretations—did the student test show how well we taught, who we taught well, and a sense of the magnitude of growth from the teaching? Same for students as the focus moved from the test items, from the score to the interpretation of the score information to help address where to move next in the learning.

During distance learning, ways to glean whether students were understanding the lesson became more complicated. However, teachers creatively innovated on ways to increase universal responses, such as using polls, chat rooms, and listening to students think aloud about their work. In addition, their students learned to digitally write their exit tickets, complete Google forms, and engage in more frequent self-assessments. When proctoring of traditional exams proved to be more challenging, educators pivoted to performance assessments and redesigned tests so that items were less likely to be readily found through a surreptitious internet search. One of the advantages of online learning is that many students are much more willing to talk (perhaps in chat to you alone or with their peers) about what they do not know, their errors, and what they are struggling with. Social media can be a great window into how they are thinking (yes, in their social life, this can lead to problems). Let's use what we have learned about the role of assessments in learning to foster practices that benefit students and educators.

REDEFINE AND REDIRECT

We think of instruction as being multifaceted. There are times when we are demonstrating a skill or concept, and other times when we are creating conditions for peer collaboration. Other facets of instruction include practice as well as the coaching and facilitating of scaffolded instruction. Assessment is equally multidimensional, and each is driven by purpose. These definitions—assessment *for*, *as*, and *for* learning—were first advanced as part of the Assessment Reform Group in the United Kingdom in 2003 and can serve as a consideration when creating assessments. Answering the question "What will I do with the assessment information?" can be a guidepost for both students and teachers.

9 USES OF ASSESSMENT

- **Assessment *for* learning:** The process involving ongoing, frequent, and purposeful exchange of information between students and teachers about student progress toward clearly specific learning goals, for the purpose of improving learning and informing instruction; formative assessment includes opportunities for students to practice and demonstrate their understanding and skills prior to summative assessment.

- **Assessment *as* learning:** Engaging students in a process of setting criteria, using self-assessment against established criteria, and goal setting, through the design and modelling of metacognitive strategies.

- **Assessment *of* learning:** Assessment experience is designed to collect information about learning and make judgments about student performance and achievement at the end of a period of instruction; maybe in the form of a grade, descriptors on a rubric or level of achievement.

Source: Edmonton Catholic Schools. AP 360 document.

Although the terms *formative assessment* and *summative assessment* are commonly used, in truth these suggest a dichotomy that isn't there in practice. Rather, think of all of these as formative and summative evaluations, with different purposes and different timing directing how they will be interpreted by the teacher and the student.

Assessment *for* learning. By far, the most prevalent form of evaluation used by teachers are assessments for learning (AfL). These are the methods used by teachers to check for understanding throughout a lesson, especially to make necessary adjustments to the pacing, examples, and practice used. As noted previously, universal response opportunities are a great way to assess for learning. Universal response opportunities are micro-assessments designed to solicit simultaneous replies from every member of the group rather than individual replies. Teachers in distance learning quickly adopted universal response opportunities using student whiteboards, preprinted response cards, polls, and hand signals to quickly gauge student understanding visually. One advantage is that these methods reduce the "follow the leader" student phenomenon of waiting for one classmate to reply before adding a similar answer (Fisher et al., 2020b). Other examples of AfL include exit tickets summarizing the lesson's learning, or to name the "muddiest point" in the lesson, that is, the point that was least clear (Angelo & Cross, 1993). We like this last one in particular because it highlights an underutilized purpose, which is to find out what students are confused about, not just what they know. The information garnered should influence what the next lesson looks like. For example, if lots of students identified a similar "muddy point," the teacher should plan on spending time unpacking the skill or concept further. If only a few students express confusion, a short, small group reteaching is warranted.

Assessment *as* learning. Assessment information should be of benefit to the student, too. Assessment as learning (AaL) approaches are designed to prompt the reflective thinking of students and contribute to their capabilities to monitor their learning. Students may be engaged in self-assessment. For example, that exit slip summary of the

> ALL OF THESE ARE FORMATIVE AND SUMMATIVE EVALUATIONS, WITH DIFFERENT PURPOSES AND TIMING DIRECTING HOW THEY WILL BE INTERPRETED.

lesson goes up several notches by asking an additional question: *On a scale of 1–4, how confident are you about today's learning?* Add a self-assessment question to the end of an end-of-unit exam: *Now that you have taken the test, what do you wish you had done more of? Less of?*

Another form of AaL are the ipsative assessments that invite students to compare their progress toward goals over a longer period of time and have them strive for personal bests. One example is having students compare an essay they wrote in the first quarter of the school year to another essay written in the second quarter. Students use the same rubric to compare their performance toward each criterion and reflect on the next steps or new goals. Ipsative assessments are sadly underused, but these, as well as other AaL tools, can promote goal setting for students.

Assessment *of* learning. Admittedly, this dimension is the one most think of first when discussing assessment; it is more the summative or confirmatory use. As educators, we are charged with formal reports of progress in the form of grades and transcripts. Many state and national exams are for this purpose, but in terms of purpose, they are quite similar to the tests we administer at the end of a unit of instruction, for a project, or for midterms and finals. While the reporting function is an important element, assessment for learning should be further used to help students notice their own learning. For example, have them sort the scored items into four categories (see Figure 10).

The purpose is for students to gain insight into what they can do next to further their learning. It can be a bit more challenging for students to look beyond the grade or score of an assessment. This process is significantly enhanced in a competency-based assessment system. We'll discuss that further in Must-Do 18.

✳ Commitments

➡ Build assessment literacy of teachers by enacting systems for assessment for, as, and of learning.

➡ Focus more on the *interpretations* from the assessments, and if there are too little, perhaps we have wasted students' time and commitments.

➡ Catalog successful assessment practices in distance learning and expand them in blended and face-to-face learning.

➡ Make sure that assessment information flows in two directions: to teachers and to students. Ensure the students can interpret the assessment information.

10 STUDENT ASSESSMENT OF THEIR LEARNING

Complex Items I Got Wrong	Complex Items I Got Right

Foundational Items I Got Wrong	Foundational Items I Got Right

What did I do well?	What do I need to practice?	What do I still need to learn?	What can I teach others?

Source: Adapted from Fisher, D., Frey, N., Bustamante, V., & Hattie, J. (2020). *The assessment playbook for distance and blended learning*. Corwin.

DESIGN AND IMPLEMENT INTERVENTIONS

REALITY

Students have needed supplemental and intensive intervention in the past and that need may be more pronounced now. Response to intervention efforts are not always implemented with integrity.

RECOMMENDATION

Develop systems to identify students in need of intervention and organize the delivery of those interventions.

When implemented with integrity, response to intervention (RTI) has a powerful impact on students' learning, with an effect size of 1.09. There are many aspects that combine to ensure that these efforts are worth the investment. The major components of this type of system include the following:

➡ **Universal screening:** A tool that identifies students who potentially need interventions

➡ **Quality first teaching:** Evidence-based instruction aligned with grade-level standards that includes systems to notice when students do not respond to the instruction

➡ **Progress monitoring:** Tools that serve as warning indicators that students are not making the expected progress

➡ **Supplemental interventions:** Targeted lessons focused on the areas of need as evidenced in the assessments

➡ **Intensive interventions:** An increase in the frequency and intensity of the interventions for a specific set of students with the most need

To put these in place, leaders must organize resources in such a way that time is allocated to the needed interventions and staff are available and prepared to deliver the interventions. In reality, lots of well-intended intervention efforts fail due to lack of coordination, not the will to provide those interventions.

> LOTS OF WELL-INTENDED INTERVENTION EFFORTS FAIL DUE TO LACK OF COORDINATION, NOT THE WILL TO PROVIDE THOSE INTERVENTIONS.

REDEFINE AND REINVENT

The first step is to resolve that your school needs a systematic model for intervention and that you are responsible for leading it. That doesn't mean you have to micromanage it, but it needs to be clear to everyone in the school that students who have unfinished learning are a priority. There is also a tendency to move students out of the class into higher tiers of support, so a focus needs to be on having professionals working with teachers to support students in the class. This resolve will be tested, to be sure, as they are likely more students in need of intervention than your resources allow. Over time, with the integrity of the interventions, this fades. But it's a common challenge when leaders initiate systematic interventions.

Next, there need to be decisions about which tools will be used. Often, school districts offer guidance on the screening and progress monitoring tools that seem appropriate. These assessments need to be administered, scored, and acted upon—both before and after intervention—to not only identify which students need deeper support but also to evaluate the impact of the intervention and ask if it is worth continuing. In fact, we recommend that you develop an assessment calendar that can serve as a checklist for these various tasks that are critically important if the interventions have a chance of working.

Then comes the schedule. Which staff members are available at which times to deliver the interventions? When are the students available? Remember that we don't want to further compromise student learning by removing them from main instructional events—so the more support can be given to the teacher to support these students in the regular class, the better for the student. There is no one action plan or concrete rules that must be followed. Take inventory of the staff you have and develop a plan. For example, in one school, the classroom teachers learned to implement supplemental interventions while the rest of their students engaged in collaborative and independent learning. In that school, intensive interventions were provided before and after school by teachers who received additional compensation for working with students for thirty minutes per day. That seems like a reasonable way to organize.

In another school, the special education teachers, library media specialist, vice principal, and trained adult tutors were used to deliver the interventions alongside classroom teachers during small group instruction. It took extra time to create a schedule so that all of the small group instruction was not occurring at the same time of day, but it seemed to work for them.

Finally, you need to monitor the impact of the interventions and adjust the plans if the systems of support that have been put in place are not working. There may be students who do not respond to the interventions. This requires you to evaluate the interventions, and if they are not working, stop them or consider that the student may need services from special education such as accommodations and modifications.

You may also be hearing about multitiered system of support, or MTSS, which expands RTI efforts and includes academic as well as social and emotional areas, including problematic behavior and other topics such as attendance. We present RTI given the effect size (there is no effect size for MTSS yet) and understand that school systems are evolving in the development of systematic intervention efforts.

✳ Commitments

➡ Develop the resolve that you must lead the intervention efforts if the efforts are to succeed.

➡ Identify and implement universal screening and progress monitoring.

➡ Develop a system and schedule for supplemental and intensive intervention.

➡ Provide training, support, supervision, and guidance for the people implementing the interventions.

➡ Monitor the impact and make adjustments as needed. Be involved in the process of determining if the interventions are working.

Must-Do 11

WIN BACK PARENT-TEACHER RELATIONSHIPS

REALITY

Relationships between some families and schools have been tested by learning disruptions, isolation from one another, and struggles with remote learning.

RECOMMENDATION

Reframe family involvement to ensure they are true stakeholders in schools.

The rapid move to distance learning has taken a toll on families, some worse than others. The twin pandemics of disease and racial injustices have cost many families and communities dearly in terms of economic stability and emotional well-being. In some places, access to technologies proved to be an ongoing and unresolved problem. Our most vulnerable students, including unhoused and foster youth, students with disabilities, and those with food insecurities, suffered even more. Even among families who had access to more supports, most would agree it has been a difficult year.

At the same time, many families have appreciated the expertise of teachers and school leaders in powerful ways. They have learned more about the language of learning and how their children struggle and deal with failure and not knowing (which are essential and desirable aspects of learning—if the work is too easy, they probably know it and need to be challenged more). They have learned that it requires skill to motivate students to engage and to persist in their learning; it takes skill to teach students to know when and how to seek feedback and then interpret and action it, and how to learn with other peers (and with, not by, parents). Expertise teachers have in buckets; it is a great time to capitalize on this appreciation and respect but also to continue to communicate with parents about their children's learning.

The measures of what schools had in the past viewed as parent participation—bake sales, classroom volunteers, athletic booster clubs—seem quaint now. They also speak to narrow assumptions about families and their resources and perpetuate institutional barriers that marginalize communities. In the same way that schools are striving to end discriminatory practices and inequities that prevent students from attainment, we must also do so with families. By interrogating the ways we welcome families (or not), work with them about the language of learning, and take actions that give families voice, we can strengthen education for all students.

REDEFINE AND REDIRECT

A deficit thinking lens is not limited to a view of students; their families often are trapped in this same spotlight. A deficit view of families is often drawn from economic, racial, and cultural biases held by educators. Families who do not regularly appear in person on campus are said to "not care" about their child's education. Those that are deemed as showing up too often, especially to voice concerns, are described as being "a problem," echoing W. E. B. DuBois's own question in *The Souls of Black Folk* (1903): "How does it feel to be a problem?"

> A DEFICIT THINKING LENS IS NOT LIMITED TO A VIEW OF STUDENTS; THEIR FAMILIES OFTEN ARE TRAPPED IN THIS SAME SPOTLIGHT.

Family involvement in the governance of the school reduces the likelihood that an echo chamber will develop because of too few voices. Schools have always had a host of committees to explore an ongoing topic. These committees often include those who advise on issues related to English learners and students with disabilities, as just two examples. Indeed, the effectiveness of schools is associated with stakeholder voice. The Consortium for Chicago Schools Research (CCSR) examined what characteristics distinguish thriving schools from those that don't. The mediators, it turns out, were not urbanicity, demographics, socioeconomic status, or the number of languages spoken.

Over a period of seven years, the CCSR examined what happened at 100 Chicago Public Schools that had made substantial gains in reading scores, grades, attendance, and family satisfaction, all while reducing educator turnover. These qualitative and quantitative data were compared to 100 CPS schools that had stagnated results (Bryk et al., 2010). What characteristics separated these schools, all of which were in the same district?

→ **A student-centered learning climate** that is safe, orderly, and attuned to its learners.

→ **The professional capacity of staff** to embrace innovation, commit to the well-being of the school, and assert a collective responsibility for every student in the school (not just those on their own rosters).

→ **Ties to families and communities** with high levels of teacher–parent trust and parent involvement in school decision making.

→ **School leadership** that values program coherence, instructional leadership, and teacher influence.

The first action to reframe family involvement is to adopt an asset-based lens about the communities we serve. This begins with investing in and expanding on culturally sustaining pedagogies and culturally sensitive programming across the organization. Educate certificated and classified staff about the community and make it clear that family involvement is everyone's job, not just that of a single committee. Keep a close eye on whether all families, especially those who are minoritized within the school, are brought into conversations about school. This may require meeting in places other than the school building, itself a symbol of intimidation for some parents. So be it.

Families should also be involved in the lifeblood of the school: instruction and curriculum. Develop tools with teachers to learn about students and their families and incorporate this knowledge into the curriculum. Host guest speakers to discuss their personal or professional lives, thereby building relevance for students' academic learning. Use many of the apps available to assist teachers in communicating with parents (search using "apps to facilitate teacher–parent–student engagement" for tools that allow you and the student to note a milestone, a breakthrough in learning, which the parents can share and perhaps talk about over dinner). Make community research a part of the curriculum. Young children can interview family members to develop a biography. Math students can learn about data collection and analysis in math by surveying family members about a topic. The intent is to make family voices come alive in the classroom.

A second action is to promote parent advocacy by providing training and sponsorships to families on leadership. Families who have not had prior experience in navigating policy, organizational structures, process decisions, and communication with government structures are disadvantaged and silenced. There are formal trainings delivered by district, state, and nonprofit agencies. While a comparatively small number of families may be involved in these, your recruitment signals an important message to all families: We need your voice inside and outside the school.

Cast a wider net by examining your communication tools to make them culturally sensitive, not just expedient. Again, these should be done in consultation with families,

FAMILY INVOLVEMENT IN THE GOVERNANCE OF THE SCHOOL REDUCES THE LIKELIHOOD THAT AN ECHO CHAMBER WILL DEVELOP BECAUSE OF TOO FEW VOICES.

FAMILIES SHOULD ALSO BE INVOLVED IN THE LIFEBLOOD OF THE SCHOOL: INSTRUCTION AND CURRICULUM.

as they are our customers. Survey families about how they receive information from the school and what is missing. Families will often remark that they actually know little about the school beyond their own child's schedule. Of course, surveys alone have their own limitations, especially for those who are already experiencing difficulties with communication. Add this as a standard inquiry item at the end of parent–teacher meetings and those meetings conducted by administrators or counselors. Ask them the following questions:

➡ How do you currently receive information about the school?

➡ How would you prefer to receive information about the school?

➡ What suggestions do you have to improve our communication?

You might add questions about their internet access, whether they use a smartphone, and what their own personal preferences are regarding how they choose to receive it (e.g., text messages, autodialer, notes home, mail).

Greater stakeholder engagement that is meaningful is crucial in a time of change for schools. Expand your ability to be a responsive leader by setting up parent advisory groups. Form advisory groups of three to eight people and meet with them at least monthly to gauge how the school's efforts are being received by constituents (so much more convenient to also use tools like Zoom for these meetings). These meetings can range from thirty to sixty minutes in length and are improved with an agenda that focuses inquiry on a particular topic, and by asking the parents to reach out to listen to others. In creating a safe space for advisory meetings, you are modeling respect and high expectations for the school community. These actions make you better prepared to be responsive to the diverse needs of students, staff, and families. Here are five agenda topics to get you started:

> **Family voice:** How do we make school a more welcoming place for families?

> **Community needs and resources:** What are unmet needs in our community? What community resources should we be leveraging?

> **Family partnerships:** What is working for you in terms of communication? What should there be more or less of? How can the school be a better partner for you and other families?

> **Equity:** What inequities are you encountering as you work with others at our school? What inequities are your children or other people's children encountering? How do we support the social and emotional well-being of parents and caregivers?

These advisory meetings can come in many forms, from Tea with the Principal to virtual meetings in the evening to an informal circle-up during a school function. One administrator we know has made a practice of hanging out monthly at prearranged times and places in front of a variety of local food pick-up restaurants and grocery stores so that families can drop by and chat. The key is to vary the times, places, and formats so that you can talk with many families.

GREATER STAKEHOLDER ENGAGEMENT THAT IS MEANINGFUL IS CRUCIAL IN A TIME OF CHANGE FOR SCHOOLS.

✳ Commitments

→ Reframe your parent involvement efforts to examine how an asset-based approach should be applied throughout the school.

→ Increase parent voice and leadership by sponsoring formal and informal opportunities for training and education.

→ Focus much of these discussions on the language of learning.

→ Strengthen culturally sensitive communication tools by asking families what they want more of and less of.

→ Expand ways in which you are seeking family voice.

12

ESTABLISH RESTORATIVE PRACTICES

REALITY

Students are punished for problematic behavior and often do not learn from their experience. They have little chance to make amends and repair relationships.

RECOMMENDATION

Develop a restorative culture that holds students accountable for their actions.

Like learning to read, write, calculate, problem-solve, and so many other things we teach, students need to develop prosocial behaviors. When we meet a student who does not yet read well, we teach that student to read. When we meet a student who does not understand how to multiply fractions, we teach that student. But when we meet a student who misbehaves, we punish that student. Instead, we need to ensure that there are learning opportunities when students engage in problematic behavior.

We recognize that classroom management is an important skill that teachers need to develop and that there are many different ways that teachers can ensure that the environment is conducive to learning. And yes, it's easier to teach in a class where students are well-behaved. Interestingly, the effect size of classroom management is 0.35, slightly below average in terms of its impact on student learning. That doesn't mean it's a waste of time to focus on classroom management, but rather that there are so many different systems and many of them are compliance focused or use shame and humiliations and thus do not result in better learning outcomes. This effect also hints that while classroom management is probably a necessary condition for learning to occur, it is not sufficient. Many orderly, well-controlled classes do not necessarily mean high-impact learning is occurring.

Pandemic teaching changed the classroom management rules. Students were simply muted if they were talking or naughty. Some students were sent outside the class, to the waiting room, or removed from the meeting altogether if they engaged in problematic behavior. Thus, the return to physical school will require reestablishing procedures and expectations. This is an opportunity to implement or strengthen restorative practices.

Advocates of restorative practices note that the shift requires a focus on relationships. It's not the rules that have been broken, but the relationships. Feelings get hurt and harm is done. Traditionally, when students engage in problematic behavior, there are punishments that students endure but they do not understand how their actions caused harm to others. When a student is punished for something, often by the administrator, victims and bystanders have few opportunities to process their feelings and tell the perpetrator how they were hurt. And the student who disrupted the learning or caused harm has little chance to make amends and learn from the experience.

> ADVOCATES OF RESTORATIVE PRACTICES NOTE THAT THE SHIFT REQUIRES A FOCUS ON RELATIONSHIPS.

REDEFINE AND REINVENT

Based on the severity of the incidence, action is taken based on the continuum of restorative practices (see Figure 11). The three foundational processes—affective statements, impromptu meetings, and class meetings/circles—mostly occur in the classroom. Victim-offender dialogue and restorative conferences are reserved for more complex situations. The skills needed for these last two processes take longer to develop, and we recommend that the initial investment of time should focus on developing the first three practices. The investment is well worth it, as regular exposure to affective statements and regular conversations with peers and adults builds student capacity for restorative dispositions. Students gain experience understanding the impact of their actions when the harm is less serious.

CONTINUUM OF RESTORATIVE PRACTICES

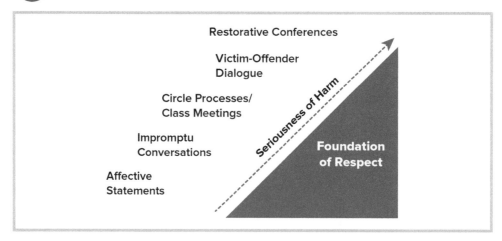

Source: Smith, D., Fisher, D., & Frey, N. (2015). *Better than carrots or sticks: Restorative practices for positive classroom management.* ASCD.

At the start of the restorative practices journey, we provide teachers with sentence starters that they can use to engage students in conversations about positive and negative behavior that occurs in the classroom. Affective statements can help with this, as is the case when teachers change from telling to a focus on the impact:

Sentence Starters for Conversations About Positive and Negative Behavior

- I am feeling distracted as a teacher by _____.
- I am so touched that you _____.
- I am having a hard time understanding _____.
- I am very pleased to see/hear _____.
- I am feeling irritated (bothered, upset, frustrated) by _____.
- I feel _____ when you _____ because _____.

Affective statements are useful in the moment, as might be the case when a student is disruptive or not engaged in the task or on a mobile phone. Other situations require a longer interaction that necessitates a private impromptu conversation. These occur when the situation is a bit more serious or when students don't respond to the affective statements. We provide teachers a few scripts for impromptu conversations that they can adapt or adopt, such as the following:

Scripts for Impromptu Conversations

- That's not the (student name) that I know. The (student name) I know is (positive attribute). Is there something that I need to know?
- The story I am telling myself about why you are _____ is _____. Where am I getting this wrong?

Key Elements for Successful Impromptu Conversations

- **Brevity:** These conversations typically last under two minutes.
- **Voice:** Students are invited to share their version of the events.
- **Honesty:** Teachers share their own feelings.
- **Accountability:** Students aren't threatened with punishment, but they are reminded that they are accountable to others.
- **Solution oriented:** Students are invited to suggest ways to resolve the problem.

Circles and class meetings can be used to address social or academic concerns. These usually have an understood structure and allow for students to voice their opinions and ideas. There is a worry that using instructional time for circles will detract from the efforts to address learning needs. In reality, the lack of a willingness to address these needs has resulted in students not paying attention to the content because they are focused on how they are feeling about something.

Circles or class meetings can focus on a feeling, such as stress about an upcoming assignment or an event that occurred, such as a disruptive class session that interfered with learning. Typically, there is a talking item and only the person holding this item is speaking. In sequential circles, students speak as it is their turn around the circle. There are other ways to engage in circles and meetings, but the key is that there is time for students to voice their opinions and work to resolve the situation.

When the situation is more serious or is repeated, leaders tend to use victim-offender dialogue and restorative conferences. These are more formal and are typically facilitated by someone not involved in the conflict. The goal of these sessions is to restore the learning environment and repair any damage done to the relationships. That's not to say that consequences are avoided. There are often consequences imposed as part of the process. It's just that many of the consequences we typically use do not result in learning how one's actions impact others. Skillful use of these formal meetings can help students change their behavior as they learn about their impact.

✳ Commitments

➡ Establish a restorative culture and philosophy in the school. This takes time and is worth the investment.

➡ Support teachers in using affective statements and engaging in impromptu conversations.

➡ Ensure victims and bystanders are involved in the process.

➡ Work to repair relationships that are damaged by problematic behavior.

Must-Do 13

AVOID STEALING THE CONFLICT

REALITY

When problematic student behavior occurs, leaders often step in and become the problem-solvers but fail to ensure that the relationship between the teacher and student is restored.

RECOMMENDATION

Provide teachers opportunities to resolve conflicts that occur.

Teachers play a critical role in restorative practices yet are often left out when harm is caused. Consider the following situation. Isaac yells something totally inappropriate in class during the time when the teacher was talking. The teacher believes that she has a good relationship with Isaac and offers a correction to his behavior. He apologizes. A few minutes later, Isaac is talking to a peer during the lesson. The teacher walks over to Isaac's desk and quietly asks him to focus on the lesson, which he does. But a few minutes later, Isaac is out of his seat, verbally confronting another student. It looks like they are going to fight. The teacher has had it and sends him to the principal.

Isaac stomps down to the principal's office. He is asked to sit outside the office, which he does. It is obvious that he is starting to calm down by the time he is called into the principal's office. The principal talks with Isaac about his actions and choices, how those disrupted learning, and how he should act instead. Isaac cries, saying that he didn't know why he was acting like that. Later in the conversation, Isaac says that his dad was deployed over the weekend and wasn't sure when he would see him again. Isaac apologizes to the principal. The principal says, "Why don't you stay here for five minutes, then go to the restroom and collect yourself? Then we need to get you back to class."

Isaac arrives back to class about twenty minutes after having been sent to the principal's office. He goes to his seat and opens his book. He is now calm and doing his work. But his teacher is not. She's still angry. And hurt. And wants to know what the consequences were for his disruptions to the learning environment.

In Isaac's case, there was restoration, but with the wrong person. His teacher had worked hard to establish a strong relationship with him. Relationships are the foundation of restorative practices. We are reminded of a situation in which a high school teacher told a student that his actions hurt her feelings. The student responded, "So what? I don't care about that." Amazingly, this teacher responded, "Then we have some work to do to get to know each other. We should care when we hurt someone who cares about us." Another teacher might have reacted differently, but this teacher understood that relationships are critical and that the absence of a strong relationship puts learning at risk.

Isaac's teacher did not publicly humiliate him or shame him. She offered corrections and private feedback. Often that works, but Isaac was not thinking about her at the time. Perhaps he did not even realize that he harmed his relationship with his teacher. He certainly did not have the opportunity to hear her perspective. Instead, disruption was handed off to the principal. And the principal solved it, learning something important about Isaac in the process.

REDEFINE AND REINVENT

We call this "stealing the conflict." The conflict was not between the principal and Isaac, but rather Isaac and his teacher. Because the conflict was stolen by the principal, resolution did not occur for the teacher. This may seem like a minor issue, but it has a significant impact on teachers:

➡ Damage to the relationship they have with the student with whom they had conflict

➡ Reluctance to develop healthy, growth-producing relationships with other students in the future

➡ Increases in the use of punitive approaches to problematic behavior

➡ Reduced agency—the belief that your actions will result in good things happening—because they no longer see a cause-and-effect relationship of their ability to impact students' behavior. Importantly, teachers with reduced agency are at high risk for burnout and job changes.

WHEN ADMINISTRATORS TAKE OVER THE CONFLICT, THERE IS OFTEN NO RESOLUTION FOR THE TEACHER.

Importantly, school leaders should avoid stealing the conflict when the conflict occurs in the classroom. If at all possible, the administrator should step into the classroom to supervise while the teacher talks with the student in an impromptu conversation. We understand that this is not always possible, that some situations require a different approach, and that sometimes the teacher is too hurt at that moment to have the conversation. But when implemented, the teacher can address the student(s) and work to resolve the issue. When this happens, all parties can move forward with learning. When administrators take over the conflict, there is often no resolution for the teacher, who might think that nothing really happened to the student and that the student got away with the behavior again. The goal is that the conflict is resolved between the people who experienced it rather than the knight in shining armor arriving to save the day.

✳ Commitments

➡ Refrain from stealing the conflict and instead empower teachers.

➡ Be willing to supervise a class so that teachers can address challenging issues with students.

➡ Create a culture that allows for relationship development, maintenance, and repair.

ENHANCE TEACHER-STUDENT AND STUDENT-STUDENT INTERACTIONS

REALITY

Teachers have expectations for students, some high but some low. And teachers are very good at ensuring that students reach the expectations that teachers have.

RECOMMENDATION

Ensure that teachers hold high expectations for all students.

High-achieving students have more positive interactions with adults than lower-achieving students—or those perceived to be lower achieving. The differential interactions are often based on the perception of the students' achievement. Low-achieving students also have fewer interactions and lower-quality interactions with adults (although students who are perceived to be higher achieving are often praised for effort and hear the message they are nice but not learners). Of course, students cannot be simply grouped into two categories: high versus low achievement.

There continues to be evidence of a Pygmalion effect in education (Good et al., 2018). The Pygmalion effect, also called the Rosenthal effect, focuses on others' expectations of a target person and the impact those expectations have on later performance or learning. As noted in Rosenthal and Jacobson's work (1992), when teachers had high expectations for students, those students performed better. And when teachers had low expectations for students, those students learned less. In other words, it becomes a self-fulfilling prophecy. A lot of subsequent work investigated different expectations for different groups of students. But as Rubie-Davies (2014) has shown, teachers with high expectations tend to have them for all students, and sadly teachers with low expectations tend to have them for all students. And both are successful at raising or lowering progress and attainment for their students. Teacher perceptions and expectations can become students' realities. It seems that the target students start to internalize the beliefs that a valued other person has about them. In some cases, it's positive, but in others, it is detrimental. Teacher expectations can be a barrier to students' learning; it's a barrier that is within our control to change.

> **WHEN TEACHERS HAD LOW EXPECTATIONS FOR STUDENTS, THOSE STUDENTS LEARNED LESS.**

REDEFINE AND REINVENT

Several decades ago, Good (1987) published his review of twenty years of evidence on teacher expectations. He noted that there were significant differences in how teachers treated students who they believed were low achieving. Good found that low-achieving students

- Are criticized more often for failure
- Are praised less frequently
- Receive less feedback
- Are called on less often
- Have less eye contact with the teacher
- Have fewer friendly interactions with the teacher
- Experience acceptance of their ideas less often

There is another term for this: a "chilly" classroom climate in which some students do not feel they are valued and instead feel that "their presence ... is at best peripheral, and at worst an unwelcome intrusion" (Hall & Sandler, 1982, p. 3). We do not in any way believe that these differential teacher behaviors are conscious and intentional. One speculation is that because educators don't feel successful with students they view as lower achieving, we subconsciously avoid contact with them. After all, we were human beings long before we became educators, and as social animals, we attempt to surround ourselves with people who make us feel good about ourselves. Students who are not making gains make us feel like failures, and so we detach ourselves even more.

Using Good's research, we created the tool in Figure 12 for you to use to assess the ways in which teachers might differentially interact with students. Remember, these are subconscious and unconscious behaviors. And even more importantly, they can be changed. Our goal is not to catch teachers but rather to help them notice and then change their interactions with students and increase the expectations they have for students. For each of the items identified below, assess the actions and behaviors you observe in class. As you do so, consider three students who are not currently perform-ing well in class.

After you have collected data across several sessions, examine it and make some deci-sions about what you need to do to support the teacher. It isn't always comfortable to look at this kind of data, but it is something that courageous educators do because it fuels improvement. As the teacher implements changes and actively re-recruits the student(s), note the change in interactions and the student(s)' learning. Talk about this with the teacher as well. Keep track of the following:

> **Patterns and trends in the data:** What am I seeing across time, across the grade level or department, or across the school?

> **Changes in identified students:** How have increased interactions impacted students and their learning? How has this changed the teacher experience?

> **Actions and next steps:** Based on the data, what do I still need to do?

✳ Commitments

> Collect data about interaction patterns and not just instructional strategies.

> Examine data for trends and develop action plans.

> Notice your own interaction patterns with staff.

OUR GOAL IS NOT TO CATCH TEACHERS BUT RATHER TO HELP THEM NOTICE AND THEN CHANGE THEIR INTERACTIONS.

12 NOTICING INTERACTION PATTERNS

Interaction	Student 1	Student 2	Student 3
Did the teacher greet the student by name when they entered the (virtual) classroom?			
How many times did the teacher use their name (not as a correction) during the session?			
Did the teacher ask them a critical thinking question related to the content?			
Did the teacher ask them a personal question?			
Does the teacher expect all or only some of the students to succeed?			
Does the teacher group by ability in the class and show that they have lower expectations of success for some of these groups?			
Does the teacher have many explanations why they cannot succeed with some students?			
Did the teacher pay them a compliment?			
How many times did the teacher provide them with praise for learning performance?			

DEVELOP EARLY WARNING SYSTEMS FOR ATTENDANCE, BEHAVIOR, AND COURSE COMPLETION

REALITY

Some students have struggled more than others throughout distance learning and are in danger of failing or dropping out.

RECOMMENDATION

Create a monitoring system to locate students in need of more support before they disappear.

The efforts of educators to locate and reconnect with students during school closures and distance learning have been extraordinary. Teachers made phone calls and sent text messages to students and families. Attendance and reengagement teams made home visits and stood outside of open windows to talk to children. There were stories of successes in working with families to encourage reluctant teens to attend their virtual classes. And in other cases, there were students who vanished altogether. Unknown economic and health turmoil uprooted some, and schools were unsuccessful in locating them.

The lists of students who needed more specialized support, whether successful or not, form the core of students who are likely to need continued care. Their return to school is likely to be rocky for them, and the habits they formed under the conditions they faced may not be positive ones. For their families, too, the routines of going to school have been disrupted. We have a good idea of who those more vulnerable students are. Enact proactive approaches to support their success and couple it with an early warning system to trigger more specialized interventions.

REDEFINE AND REDIRECT

The Early Warning Intervention and Monitoring System (EWIMS) was developed by researchers at Johns Hopkins University and the National High School Center to provide a more coherent means for assisting students who are showing a higher risk of academic failure (Marken et al., 2020). It has since been implemented for middle grades as well and is now being used in thirty-one states. The indicators fall across three broad categories, called the *ABC*s: attendance, behavior, and course completion (Davis et al., 2019). Each of these is predictive of falling behind and dropping out; the risk increases exponentially when multiple indicators are present:

> ➡ **Attendance:** The student is absent (excused or unexcused) for 20 percent of instructional time.

> ➡ **Behavior:** According to locally validated measures, the student has been suspended (in-school or out-of-school) or has received multiple behavioral referrals.

> ➡ **Course completion:** The student has failed a mathematics or English course.

We would add a *D* for *disposition*—does the student want to come to school to learn what is being taught?—as this is an early warning of the above three indicators. Jenkins (2016) has shown that from a high of 95 percent at five and six years, student disposition drops to 40 percent by the end of elementary school, as measured as those who want to come to school to learn what educators see as valuable. Also, schools can be lonely places, and making a friend in the first month of a new school year, coming back from COVID, or changing classes is a great predictor of developing positive dispositions (Galton et al., 2000).

Begin by conducting a data sweep of the last school year. Which students met one or more of these conditions previously? List those students as ones to follow as they begin the school year. Attendance is another factor that is on display from the beginning. A student who misses one day in the first week of school has already hit the 20 percent threshold. Four absences in the first month of school are further confirming. Our point is that you don't need to wait until three months of school have elapsed before identifying high-risk students.

The process itself is one that is ongoing and builds into the organizational structure of the school. Because it involves so many different educators, including teachers, counselors, attendance clerks, and instructional technology coordinators, it is necessary to formalize the process. The recommended process includes seven steps using the free down-loadable EWIMS tool guide (Therriault et al., 2013) (https://www.air.org/sites/default/files/Middle-Grades-Early-Warning-Intervention-Implementation-Guide-February-2013.pdf):

➡ *Step 1*: Establish roles and responsibilities.

➡ *Step 2*: Use the Early Warning System (EWS) tool.

➡ *Step 3*: Review the EWS data.

➡ *Step 4*: Interpret the EWS data.

➡ *Step 5*: Assign and provide interventions.

➡ *Step 6*: Monitor students and interventions.

➡ *Step 7*: Evaluate and refine the EWIMS process.

Building the team is the critical first step in the early warning system. The developers recommend that the team consist of an administrator, a counselor, a grade-level representative, a special education teacher, a mathematics department representative, an English department representative, and the school's instructional technology coordinator. This core team can set a twice-monthly meeting schedule to discuss individual students and coordinate intervention efforts. A second auxiliary team consists of representatives from feeder schools, and if this is a district effort, a coordinator; this second team should be formed to meet quarterly to consult. A general workflow throughout the school year is segmented into five major sections: before school begins, after each grading period, and at the end of the school year (Figure 13).

> **BUILDING THE TEAM IS THE CRITICAL FIRST STEP IN THE EARLY WARNING SYSTEM.**

✳ Commitments

➡ Coordinate management integration systems to coordinate data across important academic and nonacademic indicators.

➡ Diagnose and monitor the measures in the monitoring system across the school.

➡ Coordinate people and empower them as a team to make decisions about resources.

➡ Coordinate with feeder schools and the district to grow this effort.

13   AN EARLY WARNING INTERVENTION MONITORING SYSTEM WORKFLOW

Schedule	Process
Prior to the start of the school year	• Form/designate an EWIMS team (Step 1). • Provide professional development to EWIMS team members about the EWS implementation process (Steps 1 and 2). • Convene the EWIMS team (Step 1). • Set up a research-based EWS tool (Step 2). • Import or enter student information and, if available, incoming risk indicator data into the EWS tool (Step 2). • Review and interpret student needs on the basis of data from the previous year (Steps 3 and 4). • Identify interventions for incoming students on the basis of the identified needs (Step 5).
At the beginning of the school year	• Reconvene the EWIMS team (Step 1). • Verify student information, especially enrollment status, and update the student roster to reflect new enrollees, transfers in and out, and other classifications (Step 2). • Review incoming risk indicators or previous year data, including any additional information to interpret student needs (Steps 3 and 4). • Identify and implement student interventions or supports on the basis of incoming risk indicator information if available (Step 5).
After the first 20–30 days of the school year	• Update the student roster to reflect new enrollees, transfers in and out, and other classifications (Step 2). • Import students' absences (Step 2). • Review and interpret student- and school-level reports (Steps 3 and 4). • Identify and implement student interventions (Step 5). • Monitor students' initial responses to interventions in which they are participating (Step 6). • Revise students' intervention assignments as needed (Steps 5 and 6).
After each grading period	• Update the student roster to reflect new enrollees, transfers in and out, and other classifications (Step 2). • Import or enter students' absences, course failures, and behavior information (Step 2). • Review and interpret student- and school-level reports (Steps 3 and 4). • Identify and implement student interventions (Step 5). • Monitor students' responses to interventions in which they are participating (Step 6). • Revise students' intervention assignments as needed (Steps 5 and 6).
At the end of the school year	• Update the student roster to reflect new enrollees, transfers in and out, and other classifications (Step 2). • Import or enter students' absences, course failures, and behavior information (Step 2). • Review and interpret student- and school-level data (Steps 3 and 4). • Monitor students' responses to existing interventions in which they are participating (Step 6). • Revise students' intervention assignments for summer and for the next academic year (Steps 5 and 6). • Evaluate the EWIMS process, using student- and school-level reports, and revise as necessary (Step 7). • Export student data to (1) prepare the research-based EWS tool for the next school year and/or (2) share data with students' high school(s) for those students who are transitioning to high school.

Source: Therriault, S. B., O'Cummings, M., Heppen, J., Yerhot, L., Scala, J., & Perry, M. (2013). *Middle grades early warning intervention monitoring system implementation guide* (pp. 4–5). https://www.air.org/sites/default/files/Middle-Grades-Early-Warning-Intervention-Implementation-Guide-February-2013.pdf. Used with permission.

CONFRONT COGNITIVE CHALLENGES TO LEARNING

REALITY

Educators have many concerns about the cognitive challenges that students face and might use these to explain away a lack of learning and progress.

RECOMMENDATION

Confront the cognitive challenges students experience directly and develop plans to reduce the impact of these challenges.

It's easy to think that learning is as simple as introducing students to ideas and getting them to practice using those ideas. There have been many attempts at defining what quality instruction looks like, including the information in this book. We base these models of instruction on the evidence that they impact learning. But there is more to learning than simply providing students access to high-quality instructional experiences.

Learning is much more complicated than enacting good practices, in part because it is often interrupted by a range of challenges that students have experienced. Further, it is rarely linear, with students adding incrementally to what they begin with. It is more up and down, a staccato, where failure needs to be a learner's best friend, and sometimes happens in an aha! moment. Too often, we point our fingers at students' home lives or believe that students lack motivation, parental support, or innate abilities. Often, we point to things over which we have little control and instead simply admire the problem while absolving ourselves of locating solutions.

The reality is that students do experience cognitive challenges to their learning. But equally important is the fact that there are actions educators can take to reduce the impact that those challenges have. To rebound and recover learning, we need to confront the cognitive challenges that students experience and identify solutions and approaches that work.

> TOO OFTEN, WE POINT OUR FINGERS AT STUDENTS' HOME LIVES OR BELIEVE THAT STUDENTS LACK MOTIVATION, PARENTAL SUPPORT, OR INNATE ABILITIES.

REDEFINE AND REINVENT

Note that we are focused on cognitive challenges. As Chew and Cerbin (2020) note, "A cognitive challenge is a characteristic or aspect of mental processing that can affect the success or failure of learning" (p. 3). Based on their review of research, nine common cognitive challenges have been identified (see Figure 14). Note that there are specific actions that educators can take to address these cognitive challenges.

For example, let's say a student has limited prior knowledge. It really doesn't matter the reason that the student lacks this information. This lack of information will interfere with learning because we know that prior knowledge is a predictor of learning. When we build and activate prior knowledge, students learn more. The effect size of using strategies to integrate prior knowledge is 0.93, suggesting a high potential for accelerating learning. Thus, when teachers notice that prior knowledge is missing, they should be encouraged to do something about it. Given the skills that we have collectively developed with interactive videos, students could be introduced to critical information asynchronously. Or the teacher may decide that it's worth the time to have students read some introductory material to build knowledge or provide an overview of the context before beginning the lesson.

The key is to ensure that the new knowledge is gained and that spending time on building and activating background knowledge does not result in less overall learning. Yes, it's a tension, and there are many new ways to address this, given what we have learned from COVID teaching.

14 THE COGNITIVE CHALLENGES OF EFFECTIVE TEACHING

Challenge	Description
1. Student mental mindset	• Students hold attitudes and beliefs about a course or topic, such as how interesting or valuable it will be and how capable they are to master it through their own efforts. • Students may believe a course is irrelevant to them or that they lack the ability needed to learn the content.
2. Metacognition and self-regulation	• Students monitor and judge their level of understanding of concepts, and they regulate their learning behaviors to achieve a desired level of mastery. • Students may be overconfident in their level of understanding.
3. Student fear and mistrust	• Students come to a course with a certain level of fear of taking it. Students may interpret the teacher's behavior as being unfair or unsupportive of their learning, resulting in a certain degree of mistrust. • Negative emotional reactions, such as fear or lack of trust in the teacher, can undermine motivation and interfere with learning.
4. Insufficient prior knowledge	• Students vary in how much they know about course content at the start of the course. • Some students may have little to no knowledge about the content, putting them at a disadvantage compared to students with a strong background.
5. Misconceptions	• Students often hold faulty or mistaken beliefs about the course content at the start of the course. • Students may cling to misconceptions even when taught accurate information.
6. Ineffective learning strategies	• Students can employ various methods to learn course concepts, and these methods vary widely in effectiveness and efficiency. • Students often prefer the least effective learning strategies.
7. Transfer of learning	• Students can vary in their ability and propensity to apply course concepts appropriately outside the classroom context. • Students often fail to apply knowledge beyond the end of a course.
8. Constraints of selective attention	• Students can focus their awareness on only a limited portion of the environment, missing anything outside that focus. • People mistakenly believe they can multitask, switching attention back and forth among different tasks.
9. Constraints of mental effort and working memory	• Students have two major limitations in cognitive processing, the amount of mental effort or concentration available to them and the ability to hold information consciously. • Students are easily overwhelmed by trying to concentrate on too complex a task or to remember too much information.

Source: Chew, S. L., & Cerbin, W. J. (2020). The cognitive challenges of effective teaching. *The Journal of Economic Education, 52*(1), 17–40. https://doi.org/10.1080/00220485.2020.1845266

It is useful to share these cognitive challenges with teachers and encourage them to be on the lookout for each. It's especially useful for teachers to identify actions that they can take to address the challenges while still moving learning forward. We have started a list, based on the recommendations found in the research review by Chew and Cerbin (2020) and the Visible Learning research:

1. **Student mental mindset:** Explain the value and importance of the learning, increase students' ownership of their learning, and explore the habits of minds and mindsets.

2. **Metacognition and self-regulation:** Create reflection assignments, teach students about planning, monitoring, and adjusting their learning, and use practice tests.

3. **Student fear and mistrust:** Focus on teacher credibility, restructure feedback, and create a safe climate for learning and making mistakes.

4. **Insufficient prior knowledge:** Use initial assessments, provide lessons background knowledge and key vocabulary in advance, and use interactive videos.

5. **Misconceptions:** Use advance organizers, recognize common misconceptions for students at a specific age or in a specific content area, and invite students to justify their responses to that thinking.

6. **Ineffective learning strategies:** Teach study skills, model effective strategies with think-alouds, and use spaced practice.

7. **Transfer of learning:** Plan appropriate tasks, model application in different contexts, and tailor feedback to include processing of the task.

8. **Constraints of selective attention:** Increase teacher clarity, use breaks and reorientation strategies, and teach students to avoid multitasking, especially with media.

9. **Constraints of mental effort and working memory:** Organize information and chunk it, use both visual and auditory cues (dual coding), and use retrieval practice.

If teachers are able to address the cognitive challenges that confront us all in our learning, imagine how much more students will be able to do. This could be a major accelerator of learning and reduce the deficit thinking that has plagued education for decades.

WHEN WE BUILD AND ACTIVATE PRIOR KNOWLEDGE, STUDENTS LEARN MORE.

✳ Commitments

➡ Share the nine cognitive challenges with teachers and invite them to describe the ways they manifest in their classroom.

➡ Support teachers to identify interventions to these challenges and test them out.

➡ Be on the lookout for these cognitive challenges and respond to them in classrooms as you visit.

Must-Do 17

ENSURE EQUITABLE AND RESTORATIVE GRADING

REALITY

The inequities exposed in pandemic schooling include grading systems that function as structural barriers. Educators have struggled with grading practices that communicate progress but do not disadvantage students.

RECOMMENDATION

Adopt restorative grading practices that promote learning and communicate encouragement and persistence.

Inequitable grading practices have been examined and discussed in the research for several decades, yet traditional approaches remain firmly in place. Students a century ago were graded on a 100-point scale; participation, homework, behavior, and citizenship were thrown into the stew, and the averages across all were calculated to reveal a final grade. In some courses, these grades were curved to ensure an even distribution of grades, despite the fact that this is a gross misapplication of a statistical tool. These same practices continue in many school systems today. Never mind that some students are systematically being put into a hole they can't dig out of. Never mind that scores based on where a student "fits" relative to other students tell us little to nothing about growth and improvement. Woe to the student who makes a slow start early in the school year. By averaging grades, later progress is lost as the lower scores drag down the numbers. Savvy students often figure out that if they are failing in the first nine weeks of school, they are unlikely to ever make up lost ground. The system is stacked against them.

> **SCORES BASED ON WHERE A STUDENT "FITS" RELATIVE TO OTHER STUDENTS TELL US LITTLE TO NOTHING ABOUT GROWTH AND IMPROVEMENT.**

This same system is detrimental to students who know how to "do school" even if they don't master the content. The point accumulation from good participation and behavior, as well as homework completion, can obscure the fact that the student is not making satisfactory progress in their learning. The poor results they get on their tests are concealed because the overall point total is enough for them to earn credit. They earn a B- in their middle school pre-algebra class and don't understand why they fail a placement exam in high school. After all, they passed pre-algebra, right?

Grading is wrought with biases that are especially harmful for Black and brown students, English learners, and students with disabilities. Calculating homework completion perpetuates a harmful assumption that students have the time, space, and support to do so. Grading behavior is especially fraught, as it has been well-documented that disciplinary biases disproportionately affect underserved students (Skiba et al., 2014). In an effort to change disciplinary practices, many districts have adopted restorative practices that seek to manage conflict, repair harm, and, importantly, provide a space for students to learn about themselves socially and emotionally.

REDEFINE AND REINVEST

Equitable and restorative grading reform addresses three questions:

→ How do our grading practices reduce bias and remove structural barriers that impede the academic progress of students?

→ How do our grading practices foster student learning about their academic habits and dispositions and promote growth?

How can our grading practices be reliably interpreted to measure growth as well as levels of achievement over the school year?

How do our grading practices serve as a communicative tool that allows young people and their families to see progress and mastery?

Each of these questions is paired with actions to change how grading looks at your school or district. The first action is to clean up what counts in point values. Things like participation and how one's behavior contributes to the classroom climate are important but should be reported separately as a citizenship grade. Academic tasks like in-class assignments and homework are a part of practice but don't belong in measures of mastery of learning. One of the teachers we work with, who also serves as an athletic coach, likes to remind others that "we score games, not practice." Practice is an essential part of learning, and therefore errors along the learning path are inevitable. As Feldman notes, "Even though we preach, 'We love mistakes because you need them to learn!' our grading practices hang a sword above every student's head" (2020, p. 17). These tasks are collected and graded but do not hold a point value. The feedback is crucial for them to monitor their learning, but they should be monitoring their growth in knowledge, not points. A student who isn't completing their practice work is not demonstrating a satisfactory level of classroom citizenship.

The first action to take is to use summative evaluations of learning to gauge and report learning. These performance projects or confirmative exams occur at the end of a unit. Therefore, a three-week unit of instruction on the solar system or argumentative writing includes many in- and out-of-school practice tasks, but only one or two evaluation measures that come at the end. These are directly linked to the success criteria for the unit. For fourteen years, the school where three of us work has used a competency-based grading system. Students are required to achieve a 70 percent or above on each competency. Those scoring 69 percent or below are assigned an Incomplete, signaling that they have not yet demonstrated mastery. They are required to attend tutorials and engage in targeted practice work and can then retake the competency. There is no penalty for retakes (e.g., lowering the grade). There is also no averaging of competency grades. Rather, the bar is set at 70 percent for each competency. In this way, students get acknowledged for what they can do at a high level of competency.

The second action is closely related to the first. Our grading systems should be restorative in that they help the student to learn about themselves and their agency. Students who have an Incomplete meet with the teacher to discuss their plan. This provides an opportunity to discuss study habits, self-regulation, as well as gaps in academic learning (see Figure 15 for a sample contract for a biology class). Some students more frequently find themselves in this position, so there may be a more formal meeting that includes the family or other education specialists that support them. At the end of the retake, teachers ask students to reflect on the actions they took to prepare themselves and what they might do differently in the future. This is not an exercise in finger-wagging and shaming but rather a way to build student agency by letting students see how their actions are linked to results.

> ONE OF THE TEACHERS WE WORK WITH, WHO ALSO SERVES AS AN ATHLETIC COACH, LIKES TO REMIND OTHERS THAT "WE SCORE GAMES, NOT PRACTICE."

These grading reforms make it possible to communicate progress and mastery to students and their families. An equitable and restorative grading system shifts the discussion from blaming ("That teacher doesn't like me. That's why I'm failing.") while ensuring that bias is reduced. Consider this: Is it possible that the achievement gap is really an inequity gap? Is it possible that inequitable grading practices create a problem and that part of the solution is to closely examine how we report progress? Further, is it possible that reports of lack of engagement by students are due in part to the fact that our grading practices aren't restorative? We know that students who take ownership of their learning achieve. But it is up to us to make it possible for them to own their learning.

✳ Commitments

➡ Complete an audit of disparities in grading among student groups. These gaps need to be understood through the lens of equity.

➡ Work with teachers to install restorative grading practices that communicate that we don't give up on students.

➡ Meet with students and families to monitor what is working and what is not as part of your efforts to reform grading practices.

15 BIOLOGY COMPETENCY RETAKE

Student Name: _____

What is your reason for completing this form?

Check the appropriate box:

☐ Clearing my Incomplete

☐ Working toward raising my grade in the class (Example: going from a C- to a B)

What do I need to do in order to clear my Incomplete or raise my grade in the class?

Check all that apply:

☐ Science Weekly Competency: Number(s) _____

☐ Exam 1 Competency

☐ Not Guilty Project Competency

☐ Midterm

What days will I work on this goal?

Check all that apply:

☐ Mondays: Lunch (Dates: _____)

☐ Tuesdays: At Lunch/After School (Dates: _____)

☐ Wednesdays: After School (Dates: _____)

☐ Thursdays: At Lunch/After School (Dates: _____)

I understand that it is **my responsibility** to attend the agreed-to study sessions and make up the agreed-to work. By signing this contract, I am acknowledging that my current grade will be recorded on my transcript if I do not complete the contract requirements. If I fail to complete my contract obligations by the date agreed upon and my current grade is an Incomplete, then I understand that my Incomplete will turn into an F and I must retake this course to change the grade.

_____

Student Signature   Date

_____

Teacher Signature   Date

_____

Administrator Signature   Date

Must-Do 18

ENHANCE PROFESSIONAL LEARNING COMMUNITIES

REALITY

Teacher collaboration was reduced during pandemic teaching due to a variety of factors, and collective teacher efficacy may have been compromised.

RECOMMENDATION

Invigorate professional learning communities to promote their focus on their impact on learning.

There were many things that teachers missed during the pandemic, but it's possible that their professional learning community (PLC) meetings weren't one of them. Without question, there are lots of high-performing teams that continuously invest in their collective efficacy by maintaining a focus on impact. In *Rebound*, we profiled an inquiry cycle of questions (Fisher et al., 2021):

➡ Where are we going?

➡ Where are we now?

➡ How do we move learning forward?

➡ What did we learn today?

➡ Who benefited and who did not benefit?

However, there are lots of things that get in the way of teams that perform at less than optimal levels. There may be a lack of a shared vision for the team's purpose. Team members may struggle to get along and communicate well. In other cases, the team may be task oriented—just get it done—but not oriented to their own learning. Even more problematic, they may view assessments with skepticism and focus their conversations instead on blame and excuses. Under these circumstances, it is little wonder that there would be a lack of desire to reconvene as a PLC.

REDEFINE AND REDIRECT

The return to school is an opportunity to revisit the mission of what we call a PLC+ approach, and therefore **the first action**. It begins with a focus on the collective rather than the individual. With an effect size of 1.39, collective teacher efficacy is the strongest of all influences on student learning (Fisher et al., 2020a). The move to a collective requires, in part, a shared understanding of certain beliefs. These beliefs, when collectively shared among the members of the team, leverage the individual credibility and efficacy of each teacher. This is the path toward a collective. It is also not "groupthink." The PLC needs to focus their collective efficacy on the impact they collectively have on students (not curricula, but the impact of curricula on all students, etc.). There should be room for disagreement and different perspectives about data analysis and action steps. But the beliefs named here are foundational to the work of a PLC+ and are drawn from the extensive research on group processes in education. As a starting place, we offer the following statements that we believe are foundational to the work that professional learning communities must do:

> **THE MOVE TO A COLLECTIVE REQUIRES, IN PART, A SHARED UNDERSTANDING OF CERTAIN BELIEFS.**

➡ We recognize that student learning is the focus.

➡ We understand that sustained improvement requires a collective effort.

➡ We stick to what the data tell us.

➡ We accept the difficult facts and act on them.

➡ We need each other to truly address the needs of all our students.

A second action is to invite teachers to consider the characteristics of their teams and to identify areas of strength and growth opportunities. Shirley Hord (1997), who was instrumental in developing PLCs, identified six evidence-based characteristics of teams that work effectively. Each of these needs to be considered if collaboration is to thrive. While the presence of these characteristics in and of themselves won't necessarily mean a group is effective, they are important considerations that teams should discuss as they embark on the journey of improving student learning and teacher expertise. Take a moment to individually self-assess your current reality against each of the six characteristics using the rating system in Figure 16.

A third action to reconstitute and reimagine your professional learning communities is for them to analyze their recent ways of work with the inquiry cycle utilized in a PLC+ team. You can utilize the richer descriptions in *Rebound* for each of these guiding questions (Figure 17). These initial actions are aligned with the message that rethinking school lies not in the abstract but in the consequential actions that allow adults to talk with each other in ways that result in student learning.

✳ Commitments

➡ Reconstitute professional learning communities by equipping them with tools that prompt self-assessment, analysis, and discussion.

➡ Empower professional learning communities to take consequential actions.

➡ Always keep the focus on one goal: Know thy impact.

16 SELF-ASSESSMENT OF OUR PROFESSIONAL LEARNING COMMUNITY

4: This is systematically embedded within our PLC.

3: This exists but couldn't yet be considered systematized.

2: This happens randomly and is not commonplace.

1: This is not yet established in our PLC.

Six Characteristics of an Effective Collaborative Team	Current Rating			
1. **Structural conditions:** Does our team have established times that we are able to meet? Are there schedules in place that support collaboration and diminish isolation? Is there availability of needed resources?	4	3	2	1
Ideas for maintaining or strengthening this characteristic:				
2. **Supportive relational conditions:** Is there trust and respect in place within our team that provides the basis for giving and accepting feedback in order to work toward improvement?	4	3	2	1
Ideas for maintaining or strengthening this characteristic:				
3. **Shared values and vision:** Do members of the team have the same goal? Do they have shared beliefs about student learning and the ability of team members to impact student learning?	4	3	2	1
Ideas for maintaining or strengthening this characteristic:				

(Continued)

(Continued)

Six Characteristics of an Effective Collaborative Team	Current Rating			
4. **Intentional collective learning:** Does our team engage in discourse and reflection around sharing practices, knowledge, and skills to impact the growth and achievement of our students? Do we find ways to learn from each other or learn together?	4	3	2	1
Ideas for maintaining or strengthening this characteristic:				
5. **Peers supporting peers:** Does our team support lifting each other up? Do we celebrate individual and group successes? Do we observe one another while engaged in practice to help others strengthen their practice?	4	3	2	1
Ideas for maintaining or strengthening this characteristic:				
6. **Shared and supportive leadership:** Are power, authority, and decision making shared and encouraged between teachers and building leaders? Is there a positive relationship among administrators and teachers in the school, where all staff members grow professionally as they work toward the same goal?	4	3	2	1
Ideas for maintaining or strengthening this characteristic:				

Source: Fisher, D., Frey, N., Almarode, J., Flories, K., & Nagel, D. (2020). *The PLC+ playbook, grades K–12: A hands-on guide to collectively improving student learning.* Corwin.

17   TEAM DISCUSSION OF PLC+ GUIDING QUESTIONS

Similarities to Our Existing PLC Structure		Differences From Our Existing PLC Structure
	1. Where are we going?	
	2. Where are we now?	
	3. How do we move learning forward?	
	4. What did we learn today?	
	5. Who benefited and who did not benefit?	

Source: Fisher, D., Frey, N., Almarode, J., Flories, K., & Nagel, D. (2020). *The PLC+ playbook, grades K–12: A hands-on guide to collectively improving student learning*. Corwin.

Must-Do 19

PROVIDE EMPATHETIC FEEDBACK

REALITY

Teachers crave feedback that helps them grow, but many have not received useful feedback.

RECOMMENDATION

Provide empathetic feedback to 10 percent of your teachers each day.

We all want to know how we are doing and if there are areas that can be improved. Feedback is one way that we can focus on information that can be used to make changes for the better. Effective feedback can be defined as just in time, just for me, information delivered when and where it can do the most good to improve my impact on my students. There are many parts to that definition, and each is required if feedback is going to have an impact:

➡️ First, it's timely.

➡️ Second, it's customized for me based on my work.

➡️ Third, it's given to me when I can best use it, which is probably when I ask for it.

Unfortunately, a lot of feedback is given but not received. How many times have you provided a staff member with feedback, recognizing that the person was immune to your feedback? We adults are most practiced at selective listening, so it is wise to check if the teacher has heard, understood, and sees the feedback you provide as actionable. Remember, the acceptance of feedback is mediated by the relationship between the two people. And when people seek out feedback, they are more likely to act on it. Leaders need to improve the feedback they provide so that improvement remains an ongoing quest.

> **REMEMBER, THE ACCEPTANCE OF FEEDBACK IS MEDIATED BY THE RELATIONSHIP BETWEEN THE TWO PEOPLE.**

REDEFINE AND REINVENT

There is a model of feedback called GREAT. The GREAT model, developed by LarkApps, is a team productivity and engagement tool that specializes in supporting businesses whose employees work remotely but collaborate regularly. They note that building camaraderie at a distance is especially challenging and that empathetic feedback is key to high performance. And don't we want the same thing for our colleagues, whether face-to-face or in distance learning? The GREAT feedback framework consists of five facets:

➡️ *Growth oriented:* Signal one's intention as constructive and focused on improvement.

➡️ *Real:* It's honest rather than false praise as well as targeted, not holistic or vague.

➡️ *Empathetic:* Combine criticism with care and a quest for understanding.

➡️ *Asked-for:* Encourage the receiver to ask questions and seek feedback.

➡️ *Timely:* Feedback gets stale fast, so you want to make sure it is delivered soon, heard, understood, and actionable.

Let's explore empathy a bit more. Given the realities that many students and teachers faced during the pandemics, it's important to remain empathic while providing feedback. It means we need to appreciate how our feedback is being received and understood and attend to the ways that our feedback is then actioned. Can you stand in the shoes of the person you are giving feedback to and understand and appreciate how they will and do receive your feedback? Empathetic feedback is meant to be a dialogue, not a monologue. After providing the feedback, thank the receiver and ask questions that invite their input. After discussing their understanding, ask for feedback about your feedback. "Was this conversation helpful for you? Do you have advice for me about getting better at feedback?"

Finally, empathetic feedback shifts perspectives to ensure that the receiver benefits from your viewpoint while also seeing that you appreciate theirs. Once again, affective statements in the form of "I" messages are of value. Rather than voicing feedback in terms of "you" directives, affective statements frame the feedback as your own perspective. This allows psychological room for the person receiving the feedback to listen, and it reduces that initial defensive clench that might otherwise shut down the conversation before it has begun. You can use empathetic micro-feedback to make it useful and growth producing with your peers as well as your teachers.

Another aspect of GREAT feedback is to provide micro-feedback. Consider the following frame that can be used to provide feedback:

➡️ **Growth oriented**: "Here's what I would [continue/stop/start] doing."

➡️ **Real**: "When you _____, your students _____."

➡️ **Empathetic**: "We can work together on _____."

➡️ **Asked for**: "This was an area you identified for feedback."

➡️ **Timely**: "Thank you for hosting me this morning."

To increase the usefulness of empathetic micro-feedback, thank the person, include "we" statements, and obtain feedback on the feedback ("Was this useful to you?"). This isn't a script, of course, but rather a way to frame the content of the message.

We recommend that these brief feedback interactions occur regularly. In fact, we recommend that you provide this type of feedback to 10 percent of your teachers each day. In that way, you'll provide feedback at least every two weeks to each teacher. Let's say that there are 100 teachers and two administrators on a given campus. That means each leader has fifty teachers and would need to have this conversation with five people per day. If you are the sole leader of a school with thirty teachers, you would have this type of conversation with three teachers per day.

These brief feedback sessions are focused on growth. In the next must-do, we will focus on providing honest performance reviews, but this is intended to ensure that there is a focus on continuous improvement and the recognition that we can all improve our practices.

EMPATHETIC FEEDBACK IS KEY TO HIGH PERFORMANCE.

EMPATHETIC FEEDBACK IS MEANT TO BE A DIALOGUE, NOT A MONOLOGUE.

✳ Commitments

➡ Internalize the GREAT feedback model and apply that knowledge as you interact with teachers.

➡ Focus on empathy when providing feedback.

➡ Engage in these brief feedback sessions with 10 percent of the teachers each day.

Must-Do 20

HOST HONEST PERFORMANCE CONVERSATIONS

REALITY

Some teachers have not had evaluations recently, and some have not had evaluations that honestly reflect their performance in some time.

RECOMMENDATION

Engage in honest performance conversations, based on evidence, for educators.

You likely have an evaluation system that has been negotiated with a labor partner or other entity that guides the format of the evaluation and even the types of data that are included in the evaluation. These likely need to be updated as they were developed pre-pandemics and do not reflect the experiences and lessons learned during global crises of disease and the increased recognition of discrimination and racism. For example, how do the evaluations you currently use reflect a stance on equity? And do they include blended learning opportunities and the increased use of technology? Updating the tools that are used in teacher and staff evaluation is important, but we cannot wait for them to be revised. We need to act now. But our point here is that we need to be honest with people about their performance and where they can still grow. And we should expect people to be honest with us and provide us opportunities to continue to grow.

Unfortunately, lots of people (not limited to teachers) expect perfect evaluation scores. As a superintendent told us, "If they get anything less than the top rating, they are angry." They expect that their evaluation is flawless. Teachers new to the profession expect top ratings akin to the most experienced teachers. They're happy to have goals, but they have come to believe that the numbers need to be in the highest category. And we did that. Our leaders did that. They were not always honest and now have created an expectation that scores are perfect and that lowered levels suggest "bad teaching" versus opportunities to grow. When evaluations are tied with pay or other rewards, you can easily see why this would be the case.

In reality, the score doesn't really matter. What matters is the opportunity to reflect on performance and work to continually improve. We're not even sure that a numeric rating system makes sense. What does make sense is collecting artifacts about the impact of the teacher on learning, analyzing them, and identifying areas of strength and opportunities for growth. That doesn't always happen. In fact, a teacher friend of ours told us a few years ago that his principal had never visited the class—not once during the entire school year. Then, at the end of the year, the principal begged the teacher to write his own evaluation that they could both sign. We recognize the value of self-assessment, but those assessments benefit when they are discussed and the other person challenges you on your self-assessment.

> **HOW DO THE EVALUATIONS YOU CURRENTLY USE REFLECT A STANCE ON EQUITY?**

REDEFINE AND REINVENT

Good performance review systems are based on a shared understanding of the criteria being used. It's the same when using a rubric with students. If they don't understand the criteria, the tool is useless. Thus, spending time understanding what success looks like is a worthy investment. And collecting artifacts over time is important, as too many performance reviews are based on limited information. But actually, we're more interested in the performance review conversation. We have adopted the recommendations of Studer (2003), who noted that there are three types of employees:

➡️ **H = High performing**

➡️ **M = Medium performing**

➡️ **L = Low performing**

With feedback, the gap between the high and medium performers and those who are low performing widens. As demonstrated in Figure 18, without collective growth, educators hit a wall, and we all stop making progress. Studer argued that feedback is not enough to ensure that currently low-performing employees improve. In fact, he suggests that they know that they are low performing and have survived, perhaps many years and administrators, without changing. But here's an important point. We do not subscribe to the theory that you can fire your way to school improvement. We need to do things differently if we are to support all employees and their continued development. And we need to recognize the fact that some staff members' well-being has been compromised and our aim is not to increase their stress, but rather increase their sense of accomplishment.

WE DO NOT SUBSCRIBE TO THE THEORY THAT YOU CAN FIRE YOUR WAY TO SCHOOL IMPROVEMENT.

18 THE WALL

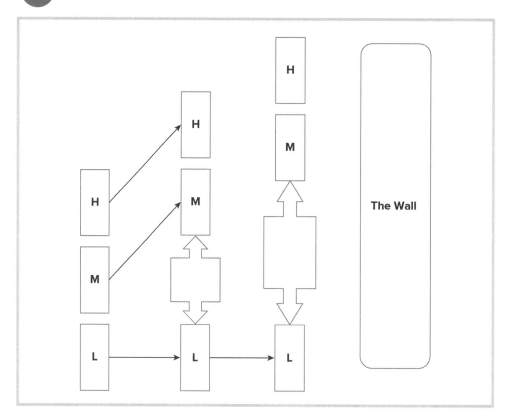

Let's start with the **high-achieving employees**. Our job is to re-recruit these staff members. They need to know that their work is valued and that their contributions are noticed. In terms of performance reviews, they already have plans for their improvement. Ask them what they are doing to improve their skillset and how you can help. High achievers want to know where the organization is going. They want to be part of something bigger. They should be tasked with serving as critical authors in modifying, if applicable, quality indicators or instructional frameworks that the school site will be using.

As part of the performance review conversation,

➡ Thank them for their work

➡ Outline why they are important and the impact on student outcomes

➡ Ask if there is anything you can do for them

The **mid-performing teachers** tend to compare themselves with the high-performing teachers and worry that they are not good enough. In fact, this is a group that is at high risk for turnover. During a performance review, reassure them that the goal is their retention. The process that helps mid-achievers grow is this:

➡ S = **Support:** Describe good qualities

➡ C = **Coach:** Identify development opportunity

➡ S = **Support:** Reaffirm good qualities, offer support, and ask what they need

The **low achievers** are a different story. Again, we are not looking to fire them. But our role as leaders is to ensure that all students have access to high-quality instruction that deepens their learning. A typical feedback session is less likely to create change. For these folks, the performance review conversation should follow this pattern:

➡ D = **Describe:** Describe what has been observed

➡ E = **Evaluate:** Evaluate the impact of the observation, such as "You did Y, therefore students weren't able to do Z."

➡ S = **Show:** Show what needs to be done and offer support

➡ K = **Know:** Know the consequences of the same performance in terms of impact on student learning

We hope that these conversations are frequent and not limited to the once-per-year (or less) formal evaluation. Our goal is to improve the experiences that all students have. Our role is to be honest and eliminate the false praise that has permeated the teacher evaluation system. We are not at all suggesting that leaders are harsh or dismissive. These are hard conversations, yet ones that can help people develop the skills they need to succeed. And we need to be empathetic in our feedback and also help teachers grow.

✳ Commitments

➡ Reach agreements about success for items on the performance review.

➡ Collect a range of artifacts that you can use in performance review conversations.

➡ Vary the conversation based on the current level of performance of the employee.

Must-Do 21
MAINTAIN YOUR SOCIAL PRESENCE

REALITY

Some teachers and staff members have not seen their leader much and feel a little disconnected. Others do not feel that they belong to a school and are unsure about the climate and culture of the organization.

RECOMMENDATION

Engage in specific actions that build the culture of the school and your social presence.

Schools have a feel, which is known as the climate. This may sound a bit offensive, but the saying in business is that "the fish rots at the head." If the leadership is not strong, the organization is probably not strong. Leaders have the potential to establish, nurture, and maintain the climate of the organization. And a positive school climate actually improves learning. The effect size of school climate is 0.43. It's well worth the investment in a leader's time.

COVID teaching radically impacted the climate of schools. Many educators taught from home, and some did not feel that they were part of a larger organization. They did not experience the same level of school spirit that permeates schools that are effective. Instead, they felt isolated, and the organization became just them and their students. In other schools, teachers were on campus, but safety protocols required changes in the interactions and routines that had once been common. There may be newer staff members who have only worked virtually and have had little contact with the wider school community. In addition, many of us experienced fear and anxiety when we were on campus, not knowing if someone there might infect us.

COVID TEACHING RADICALLY IMPACTED THE CLIMATE OF SCHOOLS.

As we rebound, we need to keep safety in mind, and we must work to rebuild the climate of our schools such that people feel that they are part of something special. We all want to know that our efforts matter, and we want to make a difference. And we want our work to be worthwhile and to believe that our organization has the right purpose.

REDEFINE AND REINVENT

Survey your faculty. There are specific actions that leaders can take to create a positive school climate for staff and students. And it starts with trust. Given the importance of trust in school climate and leader credibility, we encourage you to offer staff members an opportunity to provide anonymous feedback about trust. The tool in Figure 19 allows you to assess the trust teachers have for the principal, their colleagues, and the students and their families. The scoring key includes:

➡ Faculty Trust in the Principal: Items 1, 4*, 7, 9, 11*, 15, 18, 23*

➡ Faculty Trust in Colleagues: Items 2, 5, 8*, 12, 13, 16, 19, 21

➡ Faculty Trust in the Clients: Items 3, 6, 10, 14, 17, 20, 22, 24, 25, 26*

*Items are reverse scored, that is, [1 = 6, 2 = 5, 3 = 4, 4 = 3, 5 = 2, 6 = 1]

More information about scoring and determining where you stand in relation to other schools can be found at https://www.waynekhoy.com/faculty-trust/. Remember, these tools were developed in physical schools that predate the pandemic and the accountability movement, so take the findings with a bit of caution. Having said that, we think it's worth the effort to monitor trust as we come back from working from a distance.

Please take a moment to read this disclaimer of the Omnibus T-Scale from *Trust Matters: Leadership for Successful Schools:*

> The study of trust has been likened to the study of the roots of a delicate plant. Without great care, the examination can damage or even destroy the very thing about which greater understanding is sought. Consequently, I urge caution in the use of these trust scales. Although they can be powerful tools in helping to reveal the underlying dynamics of trust in the relationships within your school, they can do more harm than good if the information is not handled with sensitivity and care. If these data reveal that there are problems in the patterns of trust within your building, there is no better time to begin to exercise trustworthy behavior than in the presentation of these results.
>
> While these tools hold the possibility of improving the productivity and effectiveness of your school by identifying areas in need of improved trust, the revelation of distrust or even less than optimal trust, can be hard to take. Principals have described feeling very hurt and disappointed or like they have been "kicked in the stomach" on receiving results that reveal a lack of trust in their leadership. Teachers may have similar feelings. It is important not to lash out in reaction to this perceived insult. It is important to seek to understand the perceptions and feelings that are revealed on the surveys. If you don't want to know the truth, don't administer the surveys in the first place. You can be glad for the opportunity to get a window into others' thinking that might not otherwise be available to you. Suppressing negative results will only lead to greater distrust, so do not administer the surveys if you do not intend to share the results with those who offered their opinions.
>
> One thing to keep in mind about the scoring norms is that a score of less than 500 does not necessarily mean that the respondents have indicated distrust of you or others. They may, in fact, have tended to agree more than disagree with the positive statements on the survey but still come out with a standardized score of less than the mean. A score below 500 simply means that the average trust rating at your school was not as high as the average for the larger sample of schools on which the norms were based. For example, the mean score for faculty trust in the principal at the elementary and middle school level is 4.6. A mean score within your school of 4.5, or halfway between slightly agree and somewhat agree, would result in a score that was nonetheless below 500.
>
> In presenting the results of the surveys to the faculty or other stakeholders, it is important to avoid blaming or looking for scapegoats. This is the time for openness, vulnerability, and authenticity. It is time for open-minded curiosity about how things got to be the way they are, followed by a conversation about how participants would like for them to be and about how to make that happen. Compelling evidence on the importance of trust to high performing schools has been presented in this book. If your scores indicate there is a problem with trust in your building, you have the opportunity to make it a priority to address these concerns. (Tschannen-Moran, 1994)

19 OMNIBUS T-SCALE

Directions: Please indicate your level of agreement with each of the following statements about your school from **strongly disagree** to **strongly agree**. Your answers are confidential.

	Strongly Disagree	Disagree	Somewhat Disagree	Somewhat Agree	Agree	Strongly Agree
1. Teachers in this school trust the principal.	1	2	3	4	5	6
2. Teachers in this school trust each other.	1	2	3	4	5	6
3. Teachers in this school trust their students.	1	2	3	4	5	6
4. The teachers in this school are suspicious of most of the principal's actions.	1	2	3	4	5	6
5. Teachers in this school typically look out for each other.	1	2	3	4	5	6
6. Teachers in this school trust the parents.	1	2	3	4	5	6
7. The teachers in this school have faith in the integrity of the principal.	1	2	3	4	5	6
8. Teachers in this school are suspicious of each other.	1	2	3	4	5	6
9. The principal in this school typically acts in the best interests of teachers.	1	2	3	4	5	6
10. Students in this school care about each other.	1	2	3	4	5	6
11. The principal of this school does not show concern for the teachers.	1	2	3	4	5	6
12. Even in difficult situations, teachers in this school can depend on each other.	1	2	3	4	5	6
13. Teachers in this school do their jobs well.	1	2	3	4	5	6
14. Parents in this school are reliable in their commitments.	1	2	3	4	5	6
15. Teachers in this school can rely on the principal.	1	2	3	4	5	6
16. Teachers in this school have faith in the integrity of their colleagues.	1	2	3	4	5	6
17. Students in this school can be counted on to do their work.	1	2	3	4	5	6
18. The principal in this school is competent in doing his or her job.	1	2	3	4	5	6
19. The teachers in this school are open with each other.	1	2	3	4	5	6
20. Teachers can count on parental support.	1	2	3	4	5	6
21. When teachers in this school tell you something, you can believe it.	1	2	3	4	5	6
22. Teachers here believe students are competent learners.	1	2	3	4	5	6
23. The principal doesn't tell teachers what is really going on.	1	2	3	4	5	6
24. Teachers think that most of the parents do a good job.	1	2	3	4	5	6
25. Teachers can believe what parents tell them.	1	2	3	4	5	6
26. Students here are secretive.	1	2	3	4	5	6

In addition to dedicating time to build and maintain relational trust, there are specific actions you can take to nurture the climate of your school.

Rounding. Visit teachers and staff members but not to focus on the instruction. When you make rounds, you are looking to recognize what is working and improve things that are not. Try to make rounds weekly. You can ask questions such as

➡ "What is working well today?"

➡ "Are there individuals I should be recognizing?" Then acknowledge the people that are named.

➡ "Is there anything we can do better?" Take notes and work to address the recommendations.

➡ Ask, "Do you have the tools and equipment you need to do your job?" If they need something, work to obtain it.

Create a culture of appreciation. Notice things that you should be appreciative of and make sure that you recognize the effort. In fact, we recommend that you send about five thank-you notes to staff weekly. You can develop a system to do this, such as having your assistant place five blank cards on your desk every Monday morning. Write these cards (not emails) and mail them to their homes (don't put them in their work mailboxes). Name specific actions or behaviors in the recognition so that people know what you are appreciative of.

Use service recovery. Problems are bound to occur. We are in human services, and when humans interact, there are conflicts and things don't always go as planned. Instead of blaming others and thereby compromising the feel of the organization,

➡ *Acknowledge the problem*. People want to be heard. That's not saying that you are the cause of the problem but rather that you understand it is a problem.

➡ *Apologize*. In many cases, this is all the person needs to move forward. Even if it is not your fault, apologize. Remember, sorry goes a long way.

➡ *Do not manage down the organization or another person*. Don't cast blame or marginalize another entity in an effort to explain why something happened. It's not helpful to say, "That's just the way they are." or "You are the fifth person to have that same problem."

➡ *Make it right as soon as possible*. If it's within your power to change something that caused the problem, do it. If you need help from others within the organization to make it right, work to make it right.

➡ *Let the person know*. When a new system is put in place or when the wrong has been righted, close the loop and let the person who was harmed know that it has been addressed.

These may seem simple but they go a long way in establishing the climate of the school. People come to understand that their needs will be addressed and that their experiences are important to you. Yes, instructional leadership is important, and creating a positive climate that allows teachers and staff to do their work will contribute to the learning students do.

✳ Commitments

➡ Focus on relational trust within your organization.

➡ Use rounding to harvest wins and address needs.

➡ Create a culture of appreciation.

➡ Help recover from the errors in service that people experience.

FUTURE-PROOF TEACHERS AND STUDENTS

Must-Do 22

REALITY

The rapid pivot to remote learning caught educators and students flatfooted. The digital competency of teachers and students was a hard-won achievement that is endangered by a rush to return to 2019 schooling.

RECOMMENDATION

Future-proof your staff, students, and school by continuing to cultivate digital competency for all.

REDEFINE AND REINVENT

The concept of future-proofing is not a new one in industrial design and electronics but may be new to educators. The approach requires that an organization not only looks at the current landscape but also anticipates what changes may occur in the future. The result is not just speculation but rather a willingness to redesign the current product or process to ensure that it is still of value in the future. In other words, how can the organization protect itself against possible obsolescence? Schools found themselves suddenly thrust close to the obsolescence cliff when we had to rapidly shift to remote learning in March 2020. Our reliance—our assumption—was that face-to-face interactions were a given. We didn't anticipate how schooling would continue without that interface. That failure to anticipate, in retrospect, was a costly one. Teachers did not have the tools or skills to teach remotely and many students lacked the hardware, technical competence, and connectivity to do so. Schools themselves lacked the ability to function outside of a rigid set of procedures. Over time, some of these barriers have at least been partially overcome. Let's not abandon those gains with a continued assumption that education doesn't need to be future-proofed.

Much has been written about the need for what had naively been termed the skills of tomorrow. We know better now—they were actually the skills we needed today. Fullan and colleagues (2017) outlined the 6 Cs of deep learning in the 21st century—critical thinking, communication, creativity, collaboration, citizenship, and character education. We made great gains in some of these areas during the pandemic. Let's build on what we learned to foster deep learning among students and educators.

The first step in doing so is to catalog where we have made terrific gains in the last year. The first of these, without question, is in communication. Students and teachers gained tremendous digital competence at learning how to communicate with each other using digital tools. Students learned how to do file transfers, record videos to comment on their learning, and troubleshoot technical difficulties. Teachers designed robust learning management systems that kept students and their families organized. They designed and utilized digital interactive notebooks to foster two-way written communication. No child had to lose a paper or misplace their notes. Why would we go back to the way things had been? Encourage teachers to maintain and enhance communication with students and families. We have all learned that redundancy of information is crucial so that stakeholders can gain information and ask questions across platforms.

A second area of gain has been in enhancing collaboration among students. The virtual breakout rooms used by necessity during the pandemic have become a go-to means of bridging physical spaces. Students in the same class can meet in virtual spaces (a bonus when physical distancing in the room is still necessary). But challenge teachers to think bigger. Every classroom should also be collaborating with other students in the school and across the district. Build this further by fostering collaboration among educators within and across districts. One thing we have all learned is that

> SCHOOLS FOUND THEMSELVES SUDDENLY THRUST CLOSE TO THE OBSOLESCENCE CLIFF WHEN WE HAD TO RAPIDLY SHIFT TO REMOTE LEARNING IN MARCH 2020.

> EVERY CLASSROOM SHOULD ALSO BE COLLABORATING WITH OTHER STUDENTS IN THE SCHOOL AND ACROSS THE DISTRICT.

virtual gatherings of educators with similar concerns and interests have done much to amplify each other's learning. The professional generosity exhibited by countless educators has truly built a new kind of learning community that transcends job title or employer. In a field known for its very traditional hierarchy, teachers, instructional coaches, paraprofessionals, and formally named leaders have discovered they have much in common with one another.

A third area where we have made gains is in the realm of social and emotional learning (SEL) for students and adults, or what Fullan and associates call character education. Although the influence of SEL on student learning holds a high potential for acceleration, programs to build these skills were often relegated to discrete lessons in isolation of academic learning. The pandemic made it clear that the social and emotional well-being of children is inexorably tied to their academic well-being. Teachers infused their content lessons with SEL perspectives. Schools made sure that counselors and social workers met a broader range of students, not only those in crisis. The combination of an SEL-infused curriculum and increased mental health services proved to be a lifeline for many. These efforts should be continued and further enhanced.

> **THE PANDEMIC MADE IT CLEAR THAT THE SOCIAL AND EMOTIONAL WELL-BEING OF CHILDREN IS INEXORABLY TIED TO THEIR ACADEMIC WELL-BEING.**

Related to this was the discovery that the social and emotional well-being of educators was crucial. School leaders made special efforts to reach out regularly to all the adults in the building and built new procedures so that educators could talk and collaborate with each other. A real danger would be in assuming that all is well with them simply because they have returned to school. Keep these efforts in place, especially in holding regular one-to-one conversations with educators. Let's never return to the widespread perception held by many teachers that the principal only enters their classroom once a year to complete a mandatory evaluation. As we return to school, the expectation about leaders from the field is this: cultivate a caring and collaborative climate for adults.

An area of partial gains has been in the citizenship of schools. Corporations and community organizations collaborated with schools during the pandemic to mobilize hardware, software, and connectivity resources to make virtual schooling possible. We still have far to go, especially in rural areas where connectivity remains an issue and among already marginalized communities. Their suffering has shown a spotlight on the inequities that already existed. Let's use that spotlight to continue our bold outreach to community partners. Education plays an essential role in the fabric of society. Use your voice as a school leader to enhance partnerships with outside agencies.

> **THE BREACH IN SCHOOLING CAUSED BY THE PANDEMIC HAS OPENED THE CONVERSATION ABOUT WHAT CITIZENSHIP MEANS FOR STUDENTS.**

We still have far to go in other areas of the 6 Cs. However, the breach in schooling caused by the pandemic has opened the conversation about what citizenship means for students. In a year marked by pandemics of disease, social injustices, and political unrest, our children are asking hard questions about the society we are leaving them. It is clear that we must equip them with the citizenship skills that will future-proof them. We believe that these skills are the gateway to critical thinking and creativity. These round out the skills that lead to deeper learning. Importantly, it's not just children that need to learn more deeply. So do schools.

✳ Commitments

➡ Look carefully at the 6 Cs not only as a curriculum tool but also as one that has implications for adults and school organizations.

➡ Catalog the substantial gains made and continue to build on these to increase momentum.

➡ Identify where there have been some tentative steps forward and plan for how these efforts will be restarted.

➡ Look back on plans created prior to the pandemic, determine if these are still relevant, but make room in your future school plans for new things that helped students make gains during the pandemic. Prioritize these, fund these, and implement!

➡ Pinpoint where little progress has been made and marshal human and capital resources to fuel this initiative.

References

Angelo, T. A., & Cross, K. P. (1993). *Classroom assessment techniques* (2nd ed.). Jossey-Bass.

Aspen Institute. (2019). *From a nation at risk to a nation of hope.* National Commission on Social, Emotional, and Academic Development. http://nationathope.org/wp-content/uploads/2018_aspen_final-report_full_webversion.pdf

Bryk, A. S., Sebring, P, B., Allensworth, E., Luppescu, S., & Easton, J. Q. (2010). *Organizing schools for improvement: Lessons from Chicago.* University of Chicago Press.

Chew, S. L., & Cerbin, W. J. (2020). The cognitive challenges of effective teaching. *The Journal of Economic Education, 52*(1), 17–40. https://doi.org/10.1080/00220485.2020.1845266

Costa, A., & Garmston, R. J. (2015). *Cognitive coaching: Developing self-directed leaders and learners* (3rd ed.). Rowan & Littlefield.

Davis, M. H., Mac Iver, M. A., Balfanz, R. W., Stein, M. L., & Fox, J. H. (2019). Implementation of an early warning indicator and intervention system. *Preventing School Failure, 63*(1), 77–88.

Du Bois, W. E. B. (1903). *The souls of Black folk.* A. C. McClurg & Co.

Feldman, J. (2020). Taking the stress out of grading. *Educational Leadership, 78*(1), 14–20.

Fisher, D., Frey, N., Almarode, J., Flories, K., & Nagel, D. (2020a). *PLC+: Better decisions and greater impact by design.* Corwin.

Fisher, D., Frey, N., Almarode, J., Flories, K., & Nagel, D. (2020b). *The PLC+ playbook, grades K–12: A hands-on guide to collectively improving student learning.* Corwin.

Fisher, D., Frey, N., Bustamante, V., & Hattie, J. (2020). *The assessment playbook for distance and blended learning.* Corwin.

Fisher, D., Frey, N., & Hattie, J. (2020). *The distance learning playbook: Teaching for engagement and impact in any setting.* Corwin.

Fisher, D., Frey, N., & Smith, D. (2020). *Teacher credibility and collective efficacy playbook.* Corwin.

Fisher, D., Frey, N., Smith, D., & Hattie, J. (2020). *The distance learning playbook for school leaders: Leading for engagement and impact in any setting.* Corwin.

Fisher, D., Frey, N., Smith, D., & Hattie, J. (2021). *Rebound, grades K–12: A playbook for rebuilding agency, accelerating learning recovery, and rethinking schools.* Corwin.

Fullan, M., Quinn, J., & McEachen, J. (2017). *Deep learning: Engage the world change the world.* Corwin.

Galton, M., Morrison, I., & Pell, T. (2000). Transfer and transition in English schools: Reviewing the evidence. *International Journal of Educational Research, 33*(4), 341–363.

Good, T. L. (1987). Two decades of research on teacher expectations. *Journal of Teacher Education, 38,* 32–47.

Good, T. L., Sterzinger, N., & Lavigne, A. (2018). Expectation effects: Pygmalion and the initial 20 years of research. *Educational Research and Evaluation, 24*(3–5), 99–123. https://doi.org/10.1080/13803611.2018.1548817

Hall, R. M., & Sandler, B. R. (1982). *The classroom climate: A chilly one for women?* https://files.eric.ed.gov/fulltext/ED215628.pdf

Hattie, J., Fisher, D., Frey, N., & Clark, S. (2021). *Collective student efficacy.* Corwin.

Hirsch, S. (2010, September). Collective responsibility makes all teachers the best. *T3, 6*(1), 1. https://lfdev.xyz/wp-content/uploads/2010/09/collective-responsibility.pdf

Hord, S. M. (1997). *Professional learning communities: Communities of continuous inquiry and improvement.* Southwest Educational Development Laboratory.

Jenkins, L. (2016). *Optimize your school: It's all about the strategy.* Corwin.

Jones, S., Bailey, R., Brush, K., & Kahn, J. (2018). *Preparing for effective SEL implementation.* Harvard Graduate School of Education.

Kuhfeld, M., Soland, J., Tarasawa, B., Johnson, A., Ruzek, E., & Liu, J. (2020a). *Projecting the potential impacts of COVID-19 school closures on academic achievement.* (EdWorkingPaper: 20-226). https://doi.org/10.26300/cdrv-yw05

Kuhfeld, M., Tarasawa, B., Johnson, A., Ruzek, E., & Lewis, K. (2020b). *Learning during COVID-19: Initial findings on students' reading and math achievement and growth.* https://www.nwea.org/content/uploads/2020/11/Collaborative-brief-Learning-during-COVID-19.NOV2020.pdf

Marken, A., Scala, J., Husby-Slater, M., & Davis, G. (2020). *Early warning intervention and monitoring system implementation guide*. AIR.

Rosenthal, R., & Jacobson, L. (1992). *Pygmalion in the classroom: Teacher expectation and pupils' intellectual development* (Newly expanded ed.). Crown House.

Rubie-Davies, C. (2014). *Becoming a high expectation teacher: Raising the bar*. Routledge.

Segall, A. (2020). Teacher learning and the difficulties of moving civic education forward. A response to beyond the invisible barriers of the classroom: iEngage and civic praxis. *Democracy & Education*, *28*(2), 1–7.

Skiba, R. J., Chung, C.-G., Trachok, M., Baker, T. L., Sheya, A., & Hughes, R. L. (2014). Parsing disciplinary disproportionality: Contributions of infraction, student, and school characteristics to out-of-school suspension and expulsion. *American Educational Research Journal*, *51*(4), 640–670.

Smith, D., Fisher, D., & Frey, N. (2015). *Better than carrots or sticks: Restorative practices for positive classroom management*. ASCD.

Studer, Q. (2003). *Hardwiring excellence: Purpose, worthwhile work, making a difference*. Fire Starter.

Therriault, S. B., O'Cummings, M., Heppen, J., Yerhot, L., Scala, J., & Perry, M. (2013). *Middle grades early warning intervention monitoring system implementation guide*. https://www.air.org/sites/default/files/Middle-Grades-Early-Warning-Intervention-Implementation-Guide-February-2013.pdf

Tschannen-Moran, M. (1994). *Trust matters: Leadership for successful schools*. Jossey-Bass.

Index

About the Authors

Douglas Fisher, PhD, is professor and chair of educational leadership at San Diego State University and a leader at Health Sciences High and Middle College, having been an early intervention teacher and elementary school educator. He is the recipient of an International Reading Association William S. Grey citation of merit, an Exemplary Leader award from the Conference on English Leadership of the National Council of Teachers of English, as well as a Christa McAuliffe award for excellence in teacher education. He has published numerous articles on reading and literacy, differentiated instruction, and curriculum design, as well as books, such as *PLC+: Better Decisions and Greater Impact by Design, Building Equity*, and *The Distance Learning Playbook.*

Nancy Frey, PhD, is a professor in educational leadership at San Diego State University and a leader at Health Sciences High and Middle College. She has been a special education teacher, reading specialist, and administrator in public schools. Nancy has engaged in professional learning communities as a member and in designing schoolwide systems to improve teaching and learning for all students. She has published numerous books, including *The Teacher Clarity Playbook* and *The Distance Learning Playbook.*

(Continued)

Dominique Smith, EdD, is a social worker, school administrator, mentor, national trainer for the International Institute on Restorative Practices, and member of Corwin's Visible Learning for Literacy Cadre. He is passionate about creating school cultures that honor students and build their confidence and competence. He is the winner of the National School Safety Award from the School Safety Advocacy Council. Dominique's major area of research and instruction focuses on restorative practices, classroom management, growth mindset, and the culture of achievement. He earned his master's degree in social work from the University of Southern California and his doctoral degree in educational leadership at San Diego State University.

John Hattie, PhD, is an award-winning education researcher and best-selling author with nearly 30 years of experience examining what works best in student learning and achievement. His research, better known as Visible Learning, is a culmination of nearly 30 years synthesizing more than 1,500 meta-analyses comprising more than 90,000 studies involving over 300 million students around the world. He has presented and keynoted in over 350 international conferences and has received numerous recognitions for his contributions to education. His notable publications include *Visible Learning, Visible Learning for Teachers, Visible Learning and the Science of How We Learn, Visible Learning for Mathematics, Grades K–12,* and, most recently, *10 Mindframes for Visible Learning.*

A SAGE Publishing Company

Helping educators make the greatest impact

CORWIN HAS ONE MISSION: to enhance education through intentional professional learning.

We build long-term relationships with our authors, educators, clients, and associations who partner with us to develop and continuously improve the best evidence-based practices that establish and support lifelong learning.

The PLC+ Books

Corwin's PLC+ framework is aimed at refreshing current collaborative structures and helps support teachers' decision making in the context of individual and collective efficacy, expectations, equity, and the activation of their own learning. The PLC+ books provide a foundation for this critical work.

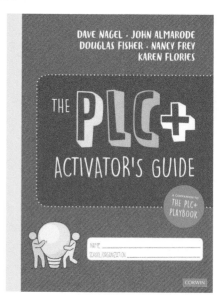

PLC+

Better Decisions and Greater Impact by Design

What's this book about?

- Provides a brief history of PLCs

- Introduces the PLC+ framework questions and crosscutting themes

- Shows the PLC+ in action in various settings

When do I need this book?

- You want to understand the purpose of PLCs

- You want to learn a new framework for effective PLCs

- You want to reinvigorate and increase the impact of your existing PLC

The PLC+ Playbook

A Hands-On Guide to Collectively Improving Student Learning

What's this book about?

- Provides a practical, hands-on guide to implementing the full PLC+ cycle

- Guides PLC+ group members through 22 modules as they answer the five guiding questions and focus on the four crosscutting themes

- Offers modules comprising an array of tools that support implementation of the PLC+ framework

When do I need this book?

- You want to plan and implement the PLC+ framework in collaborative settings

- You want to implement the PLC+ model step by step in your own PLC

The PLC+ Activator's Guide

What's this book about?

- Provides guidance for the PLC+ team activators

When do I need this book?

- You are a PLC+ activator and want to do the best possible job for your group

- You are an activator and want to pre-plan the implementation of your PLC+

- You need help to guide the group in overcoming obstacles or having difficult conversations

PLCN21241